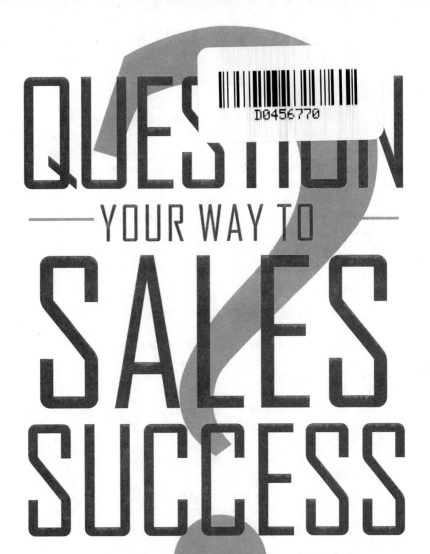

QUESTION
— YOUR WAY TO —
SALES
SUCCESS

Gain the Competitive Edge and Make
Every Answer Count

DAVE KAHLE

CAREER
PRESS

Franklin Lakes, NJ

QUESTION YOUR WAY TO SALES SUCCESS
EDITED AND TYPESET BY KARA REYNOLDS
Cover design by Rob Johnson/Johnson Design
Printed in the U.S.A. by Book-mart Press

To order this title, please call toll-free 1-800-CAREER-1 (NJ and Canada:
201-848-0310) to order using VISA or MasterCard, or for further information on books from Career Press.

The Career Press, Inc., 3 Tice Road, PO Box 687,
Franklin Lakes, NJ 07417
www.careerpress.com

Library of Congress Cataloging-in-Publication Data
Kahle, Dave.
   Question your way to sales success : gain the competitive edge and
make every answer count / by Dave Kahle
      p. cm.
   Includes index.
   ISBN 978-1-56414-994-7
      1. Selling. 2. Sales management. I. Title.

HF5438.25.K338 2008
658.85--dc22

                                                        2008005643

Question
Your Way to
Sales
Success

Acknowledgments

I'm sometimes asked, "How long did it take you to write the book?" The answer is the same for this book as it has been for earlier books: In one sense, a few months; in another, my entire life.

The material in this book has been influenced by countless interactions throughout the course of my life.

Way back in my days as a university student in the college of education, I was first alerted to the potential power of an appropriately phrased question to direct a student's thinking.

In my 40-plus years as a professional salesperson, I've had a nearly unlimited number of interactions with customers, during which I've honed many of the observations and insights contained in this book.

The authors who have gone before me and addressed this topic in earlier works have helped shape my ideas.

Certainly, all the salespeople who have developed and submitted questions in my seminars and training programs have had an enormous impact on the book.

Cheryl Cochran, my administrative assistant, helped me attend to the details.

My wife, Coleen, has supported me in my choice of a career, and accepted all the implications of that.

Undergirding all of these experiences and influences has been the impact of Jesus Christ on my life. It has been my relationship with Him that has brought purpose and direction into my life and work.

Contents

Introduction

I was educated as a teacher, and during my entire secondary education I pursued the study of how people think and learn. Throughout my career as a professional salesperson, that subject continued to intrigue me. I have read almost everything written on the subject, and tested many practical ideas in my seminars and training programs.

In the last 20 years, my focus has been on training salespeople and sales managers to become more effective. It has always seemed to me that there was a natural point at which effective thinking intersected with effective sales. The best salespeople are great thinkers.

I have come to understand that an effectively phrased question is the ultimate thinking tool. In fact, it may be that all good thinking begins with a question. All of our focused attempts to think through to a decision are ultimately attempts to answer questions. For example, we may think, "What should I do?" Or, "Should I go here or there?" "Should I marry John or Tom?" "Should I take this job?"

The questions we create dictate the focus of the thinking that follows. That is true for every personal and business circumstance. And it is especially true for salespeople.

But the power of a question to focus and energize thinking isn't just limited to our own thoughts. It is the most powerful tool a salesperson has to influence and energize the thinking of our customers as well.

The ability to create and deliver a series of penetrating and revealing questions is an essential competency for professional salespeople. Every salesperson can ask a question, but very few consistently ask good questions. And no one is as good as he or she could be at this competency.

Throughout the 20 years in which I have been educating salespeople, the training I present on the skill of asking questions has consistently been the best received, most highly praised, and most intensely behavior-changing of all the topics on which I speak. This is true whether it be a 60-minute module in a larger program, or a full-day program dedicated entirely to the issue.

That says that there is a huge need for better performance on this issue.

In this book, I share with you the insights I have gained in a lifetime of study of effective thinking, and, specifically, effective questions. The book is designed to provide professional salespeople with the principles, processes, practices, and tools that will empower them to ask better questions, both of themselves and of their customers, and thus dramatically affect their sales results.

The book is also designed as a tool for sales managers to encourage and coach their salespeople toward the same end. And it has application for other professions, as a stimulant toward the more effective use of questions to help clients achieve their goals.

One particular feature is the analysis of real questions proposed by real salespeople in real sales calls. One of the most popular portions of my seminars occurs when I assemble the participants into small groups, and task them with creating a series of questions for a specific sales opportunity. We then listen to the questions each group has produced, and comment on the language in those questions. It's that process that provides the fodder for the "review" sections in most chapters in this book.

Enjoy!

The Question
Is the Key

Focus, focus, focus. That's the phrase I find myself repeating constantly in every sales seminar I present. I believe focus is the greatest challenge for salespeople today, and the greatest single solution to their challenges. There are so many demands on our time, so many tasks calling for our attention, and so many opportunities available to us that we can easily become scattered and dissipated.

As a result, we squander our energies on tasks of little effect, and, at the end of the day, are exhausted, too often having accomplished little of any importance. We complain about being overworked, and we're irritable and haggard, all because of our inability to focus.

Focus means "to give your main attention to one thing." In this age of sound bytes, video games, instant messages, and cell phones, the ability to focus our attention on one thing is becoming rare. We consider ourselves multitaskers, instead of one-taskers. Multitasking is a great way to accomplish a lot of little things, whereas one-tasking is a far more effective way to accomplish something meaningful.

Remember the movie *City Slickers*, in which Billy Crystal asked Curly what was his secret? He held up one finger and said, "One thing." Focus on doing one thing well.

The job of the salesperson is a sophisticated challenge that will require the best we have in order to master it. And that means that we must focus our energies and strengths on those tasks that will bring us success.

The rewards are worth it. As successful salespeople, we can expect to be in the group of more highly compensated people in this world. There are millions of people who would love to have our jobs. As we develop a pattern of success, that pattern provides us a level of job security. Not only are we valuable to our companies, but our resume also makes us attractive to others. Good salespeople are always in demand.

But the rewards go beyond the financial. Success at sales requires that we develop our people skills. And as we gain competency in dealing with all kinds of people, we naturally use these skills in relationships and transactions beyond our customers. We become more adept at dealing with relatives, friends, neighbors, and so on. The organizational and thinking skills we develop likewise spill over into our personal lives and help us to become successful in whatever group, hobby, or affiliation we choose.

And all of this together helps nurture within us a sense of confidence. That confidence is immensely attractive to others around us, making us a source of influence to our acquaintances.

All of this is a result of our ability to focus. But our focus can be wrongly directed—it is possible to focus on the wrong things. If, for example, you choose to focus on memorizing all the esoteric details and specifications of your product, you will become successful at knowing those. However, your focus will have been wrongly focused for success at sales.

It is necessary, therefore, to rightly focus. Yes, in sales there is right and wrong, appropriate and inappropriate, wise and foolish.

In my 40-plus years of experience in the sales profession, I have identified several places at which focus will gain you the greatest results. At the top of the list is focusing on the skill of asking better sales questions.

If there is only one practice within the scope of the professional salesperson upon which you can focus, let it be to gain mastery in asking better questions.

Let me repeat that, just to make sure that you get it: If there is only one practice within the scope of the professional salesperson upon which you can focus, let it be to gain mastery in asking better questions.

As you read the rest of this book, you'll see why a question is such a powerful sales tool. For now, however, let's start with this observation: A series of better sales questions provides you leverage and a competitive edge at every stage of the sales process.

Of all the things you can do and say when you are talking with a customer, there is none that even comes close to the power of asking a good question. It stands alone, apart from every other tactic, as your single most powerful sales tool. Nothing even approaches it.

Of all the ways you can think about your job, nothing comes close to formulating powerful questions to ask yourself, and then answering them in writing. The question you ask yourself is your single most powerful thinking tool.

That power springs from a simple principle: *When you ask a question, they think of the answer.* I know that sounds incredibly basic, but the most powerful truths are often thus. If you consider this, you'll come to the conclusion that the language in your question influences, shapes, and energizes the thinking of the person to whom the question is asked.

In the case of asking the customer, the question influences, shapes, and energizes the thinking of your customer. Not only that, but the language in the questions you ask yourself also directs and focuses your own thinking.

Where does the decision to buy your product or service ultimately take place? Isn't it in the mind of the customer? And what one tool allows you to shape what takes place in that mind? A good question.

Let me prove it to you. Answer this question: Did you enjoy what you had for breakfast this morning? Now consider what you did when you read that question. Probably, in a split-second spent thinking, you conjured up a picture of you eating breakfast this morning. You reviewed that by considering the picture, and then made a judgment about it: You either did or did not enjoy it. In other words, my question caused you to think a certain way, about a certain subject. And every person who reads this book will do exactly the same thing. My question will direct and influence the thinking process of thousands of people in some small way.

Our natural reaction, when we are asked a question, is to think of the answer. While it is possible to be asked a question and not think of the answer, it generally takes some planning and an act of willpower to do so. Even then, our conditioning often takes over and supplants our intentions. For example, decide, right now, not to think of the answer to this question. I'm going to ask you a question, but I want you to *not* think of the answer. Ready? *How old are you?*

Don't think of the answer!

If you are like most people, by this point the answer has crept into your mind and oozed out into your consciousness.

That's the ultimate power of a question. When someone asks a question, you think of the answer. These two questions

I just asked were, both, relatively trivial. Imagine, however, the power of a more significant question—or, better yet, a series of significant questions—to direct and influence the thinking of your customers. Are you beginning to gain a sense of the tremendous power of a question?

Here's an example of how this operates in a practical selling situation: You've just made a proposal or a presentation of your solution. You ask the customer,

? What do you not like about my product? ?

That's a terrible question. What is the customer going to think about as a result of your question? All the faults he can find with your product.

On the other hand, you could influence the customer to think much more positively about your product by asking this question:

? In what ways do you see yourself (or your company) benefiting from this product?

I'd much prefer to have the customer think about the answer to the second question, rather than the first. In this scenario, it was your question that influenced the direction of the customer's thinking. That's the ultimate power of a good sales question.

We're going to be considering two basic types of questions: Questions you ask customers and prospects, and questions you ask yourself. We'll call the first set *sales questions*, and the second *self-questions*.

The power of a question to direct thinking applies just as powerfully to you. When you ask yourself questions, you direct, influence, and energize your own thinking.

My work with questions has led me to conclude that the question is your most powerful thinking device, shaping and prompting excellent analysis, great prioritizing, powerful creativity, and excellent plans.

Your ability to think well depends on the language in the questions you ask yourself. Here's an example: At one time, I sold for a distributor of hospital supplies. I was instructed by my manager to make sure that I always had something to present to every customer on whom I called. I thought he probably knew what he was doing, and I followed his direction. Every time I mentioned a product line I carried, or handed over a piece of literature, or provided a sample, or demonstrated a product, I'd call that a "sales presentation." Thus, I was prepared to make a sales presentation on every sales call. At some point along the way, I thought that if I could increase the quantity of sales presentations I made, I could probably correspondently increase the number of opportunities I uncovered, and thus, eventually, the volume of my sales. So I asked myself this question:

> *Great Question*

> **? How can I double the quantity of sales ?**
> **presentations I make in my territory?**

The answer to the question was obvious: Take two things with me on every sales call. Although the answer was obvious, it took asking the right question to uncover that answer and the resulting strategy. I determined to do just that, and saw my sales increase dramatically.

Some time later, I asked myself a similar question:

> **? How can I increase the quantity of sales ?**
> **presentations I make in my territory?**

Again, the answer was obvious: Take more than two! The answer was lying there for everyone to see. But it took the right question to uncover it. It wasn't until I asked the right question that I discovered the resulting strategy.

So, again, I implemented that strategy and saw my sales increase again.

Some time later, I asked myself a different question:

? How can I cause the quantity of sales presentations in my territory to be increased?

Great Question!?

Notice the difference in the language of the question. Now, it wasn't just about me. Because I asked the question in a different way, it led me to a different answer, and a different strategy.

What was the answer to the most recent question? I could influence some of the manufacturer's representatives who sold the lines I carried to work on my behalf in my territory. If one of them made a product presentation in my territory, it would have the same effect as if I had made it myself. So, I determined to identify, and then work with a core group of manufacturer's reps, with whom my company had exclusive relationships, and whom I determined to be competent, honest, and reliable sales reps.

What was the eventual outcome of this strategy? I did five times the volume of the average rep in that field.

Notice the sequence of events. Let's start at the end: I did huge volumes of business—five times the amount of the ordinary sales rep. One of the reasons I did that kind of volume was that I created more opportunities than anyone else. One of the reasons I generated more opportunities was my routine of working closely with a core group of manufacturer's reps, and thoroughly preparing to show several items to every prospect or customer in every sales call. I implemented those strategies because I arrived at the obvious answer to some questions I asked myself.

What were the stimuli that created this whole sequence of events? They were the questions I asked myself.

As we consider several common selling situations, we'll be looking at self-questions as well as sales questions.

The Power of a Good Sales Question

The power to direct and influence a customer's thinking is the primary function of a good question, but it is certainly not the only benefit. Let's look at some of the other benefits of asking good sales questions.

1. A series of good questions is your primary tool for collecting deeper and more detailed information about the customer.

This is the classic benefit most people would put first on a list. However, most salespeople, although they may realize the importance of this benefit, don't implement it with excellence.

It is one thing to ask questions to collect information, and it's another to ask deeper questions and collect more significant information.

Collecting information about your customer is like peeling an onion.

Suppose you've just come back from your company's annual sales meeting. For three days, you sat in meetings and ate hotel food. Now, you're home, and you'd like nothing more than a cold beer and a home-cooked meal. You suggest a big salad for dinner, and your spouse agrees, suggesting that you peel the onion.

So you get out a big, fat, Bermuda onion—about the size of a softball. You position it carefully on a cutting board, and root through the drawer until you find a sharp meat cleaver. Steadying the onion with one hand, you raise the meat cleaver above your head, and, with a karate-type movement, smash the meat cleaver neatly into the center of the onion, splitting it evenly in half. You pick up one of the onion halves and examine it from the inside. You note that it has layers and layers, each deeper and more tightly compressed than the one surrounding it. You begin to peel the onion, stripping off the skin. As you pull off the skin of the onion, you notice that the skin is thin, dry, and crinkly, with very little scent. As you peel each layer, one at a time, you soon come to the conclusion that each layer is more strongly scented than the one before it, and that the strength of the onion's pungency comes from the inside out. Got the image?

Good. That's the best way to understand this principle. Just as there are layers to an onion, so there are layers to your customer. Just as the superficial layers of an onion are thin and mild, so too the superficial levels of your customers have little strength. But as you peel the onion deeper, the strength increases. So too it is with your customer.

Let's apply this specifically to understanding your customer in a sales situation. Look at Illustration 1. Imagine it to be a slice of that onion. On the very surface are the technical specifications for the product or service the customer wants.

For example, let's say you call on one of your customers, and she says, "I need to purchase three green metal widgets that are 1/2 inch by 6 inches. Many salespeople would say, "Okay, they are $2.50 each." In this example, the salesperson understood the customer at the most superficial level—technical specifications—and responded in kind.

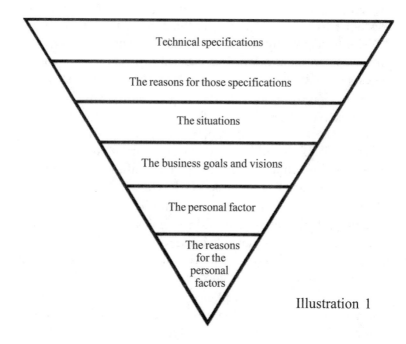

Illustration 1

Peeling the onion

But you can go deeper in understanding the customer by discovering the reason behind those specifications.

Our rep, when confronted with the same request, may say, "What are you going to use them for?" or, "Is there a reason you asked for metal instead of plastic?" This kind of response will uncover the next level, the *reason* for the specifications.

There's more. *Situation* refers to the history behind the need, and the circumstances surrounding the need. For example, let's say our salesperson now replies, "John, what's your situation? Why is this an issue now?" When the customer replies to that question, the salesperson has uncovered a deeper layer of need.

Yet you're still pretty close to the surface. When you uncover the specific problems and objectives that underlay the original request, you've gotten deeper in your understanding of the customer. Back to our example. Suppose your customer says, "We're having a problem with our second-shift production. The line keeps breaking down. Our maintenance supervisor wants to stockpile some of the parts he has been regularly replacing."

Now you have an understanding of the specific problems and objectives. There is more. Suppose you ask how that problem affects the rest of the company. And suppose your customer explains the effect of the breakdown on production, net profits, and overtime pay for the second shift. Now you understand the customer at yet a deeper level.

But you can go deeper still. When you ask how those systematic problems affect his business goals, and you learn that it's particularly troublesome because your customer's goal is to increase net profits by five percent this year, you understand the customer at an even deeper level.

You take a significant plunge deeper when you are able to understand how the situation affects the individual with whom you're talking. For example, when you know him well enough to ask, "John, how can I make you look good in this transaction?"

and get an honest response, you've penetrated to a new layer of understanding.

Finally, when you understand the individual motivations—the reasons for the personal factors—you understand the customer at levels few salespeople ever approach. That's where the masters work. Those motivations are often emotionally driven. So when you understand the customer's emotions—how the situation makes him or her feel—you've arrived at the heart of the onion.

Collecting information at deeper levels—peeling the onion—is one of the most powerful functions of a series of good questions.

2. A series of good questions is a powerful way to enhance a relationship.

Did you ever meet someone in a social setting, and that person seemed particularly interested in you? She asked about you, where you lived, what you did, what hobbies you pursued, your family, and so on. And then, after chatting so agreeably for a while, you both went on to other conversations. Afterward, you reflected on the exchange and thought to yourself, "What a nice person."

What made you think she was a nice person? Clearly, it was that she was so interested in you. And what made you think she was interested in you? The series of questions she asked about you.

The questions functioned as a mechanical device—a key—that unlocked positive feelings toward the other person on your part.

3. A good question can create insights on the part of the customer.

An insight is a new realization on the part of the customer of some priority or value of which he was previously not aware.

Here's a great example. A couple of years ago, my wife and I were shopping for a car for her. In this process we encountered a number of automobile salespeople. Eventually, we came across a good one. I knew he was a good salesperson because he took the time to discover our needs and interests before launching into a dumping of all the features of a particular automobile. He asked good questions.

Here was the one I remember: After he discovered that we were looking for a car for my wife, he directed his questions to her. He asked, "Mrs. Kahle, which would you rather have—a car that is sporty and quick and fun to drive, or one that is more stable and comfortable?"

She thought for a moment, and replied, "Well, I've had sporty, so I think I'm ready for comfortable."

She did not know that prior to being asked the question. But as a result of a good question asked by a good salesperson, she processed life experiences, values, and feelings, and formulated a reply. And when that reply turned into words and came out of her mouth, she knew what she wanted. The question helped her gain an insight into her own values and interests.

The salesperson, in addition to moving the sale forward, did us a service by asking a good question to help clarify our values.

4. A series of good questions is a powerful way to create the perception of your competence in the mind of the customer.

Do you want your customers to think of you as a competent person whom they can trust? Of course you do. Your position in the mind of the customer is crucial to the development of the sale. How do you position yourself as competent in the mind of the customer? One way is to ask a series of good questions.

For example, let's say you are having trouble with your car, and you take it to a mechanic. He has a big neon sign in the window proclaiming "Computer Diagnostics." You tell him your problem: "The car is making a weird noise." He says, "We have computer diagnostics here. Leave it with me and pick it up at 5 p.m." You're not quite sure you are ready to do that, so you go across the street to the mechanic on the other side of the street.

You say the same thing to him: "The car is making a weird noise."

He asks, "What kind of noise?"

You reply, "A weird thumping sound."

"Where is it coming from?"

"The front of the car."

"Driver's side or passenger's side?"

"Passenger's side."

"What are you driving?"

"A 2005 Taurus."

"Okay, when you start the car in the morning, and the engine is cold, do you hear the sound then as loudly and as frequently as you do later in the day when the engine is warm?"

You think for a moment, and then reply, "No, I don't. It is always louder and more frequent later in the day."

He considers for a moment and then asks you, "And when you drive down the road at different speeds, do you hear the sound more frequently as you drive faster, and less frequently when you drive slower?"

You reply, "Yeah, that's exactly what happens."

He says, "Okay. Leave it here with me, and pick it up at 5 p.m."

With which of those two mechanics do you leave your car? Almost everyone with whom I use this example answers without hesitation, the second mechanic. Why is that? Because he knew what he was doing. And what did he say to indicate to you that he knew what he was doing? Nothing. He said nothing. But he did ask a series of questions. And you formed your opinion of his competence, not by what he said, but rather by what he asked.

There is something in our human natures that understands that it takes more competence with a subject area to be able to ask good questions about it than it does to talk about it.

5. A series of good questions is the best way to uncover concerns in your customer.

Rarely does your proposal allay every concern in the customer's mind. After first being exposed to your solution, the customer often has concerns about some aspects of your offer. Very frequently, the customer won't proactively volunteer these questions and concerns. You need to uncover them with a series of good questions.

For example, you have just presented your new software solution, offered to meet the customer's need for a more detailed customer-relationship-management package.

You ask a series of questions such as these:

? How do you feel this fits with your situation? **?**

? To what degree are you comfortable with this solution? **?**

? What questions or concerns have you about this? **?**

Those questions, and others of a similar nature, will uncover any remaining issues so that you can work to resolve them.

In this example, let's say that your customer, in response to the first question, responds this way: "It looks like it does everything we want it to do. I'm just a little concerned about how quickly our salespeople will be able to implement it."

Very likely, you would not have known about that concern in the customer's mind if you had not asked the question. But you did ask the question, and in so doing you uncovered a concern in the customer's mind that may have been a deal-breaker.

Now that you know about that concern, you can address it and, thus, move the sale one more step toward completion.

6. A good question is your primary tool for gaining agreement with the customer.

Coming to some agreement with the customer is the purpose of every sales call. That doesn't mean that every call should result in a purchase order. That may be the ultimate goal, but it is unrealistic in most selling situations to expect it. What is appropriate, however, is to expect that there will be some agreement with the customer every single time you call on her.

For example, if you call someone for an appointment, you expect to agree on a time and date to meet. A simple question such as,

> ? Which is better for you, Monday at 2 p.m., ?
>   or Tuesday at 10 a.m.?

will put the issue directly in front of the customer.

If you make a cold call on a prospect, you ought to attempt to get an agreement to see you again. A question such as,

> ? Sounds like we should get together next month. ?
>   Which day works best for you?

will get this process moving to agreement.

If you collect information about a specific opportunity, the customer should agree to consider your proposal. You could ask something similar to this:

? I'll have the proposal ready for you in about a week. **?**
When should we meet to review it?

If you make a proposal, the customer should agree to meet with you to discuss his concerns. Use a question similar to this:

The next step is probably exploring your concerns and questions.

? Shall we get together with that agenda? **?**

If you negotiate with the customer, you should expect a commitment to try or buy the product. You could use simple closing questions such as,

? Do you want to go ahead with this? **?**

On and on it goes. You use questions—your most power-ful sales tool—to gain agreement with the customer at every step of the sales process. Without asking the question, you rarely gain agreement, because you don't put the issue on the table in front of the customer. Questions are your most powerful tool to move the sale forward, from one agreement to the next.

The question is the key

At every stage of the sales process, a good sales question, or a series of good sales questions, is your most powerful tool to accomplish that step of the sales process. Think of a good question as a powerful key that unlocks deeper and richer re-sponses from the customer at every step in the process.

Your ability to quickly and effectively move a sufficient number of customers through the sales process is the essence of selling. Your ability to master the use of good questions is your most powerful tool. The rest of this book will set you well on your way to achieving that mastery.

A Better Sales Question

3

Are you the decision-maker on this issue?

That's a poor question, because it violates one of our criteria for a good sales question: It may cause the customer to lose face. If he says no, he may have lost a little standing in your eyes. Better to ask,

Who, besides yourself, will be involved in this decision?

That will yield the same information, but protect the customer's ego.

That's an example of an incredibly powerful observation: Everyone can ask questions, but the best salespeople consistently ask *better* questions. There is such a thing as a better question.

A number of years ago, the National Society of Sales Training Executives published the results of a survey it had done in an attempt to identify the characteristics of the best salespeople. The society studied salespeople from a wide variety of selling situations and industries in order to gain a broader picture of the makeup of a superstar salesperson.

The results of the survey? The best salespeople, regardless of what they sell or to whom they sell it, "see the situation from the customer's point of view," "ask better questions," and "listen more constructively."

Notice the relationship among these top three characteristics. What gives these superstar salespeople their competitive advantage? They see the situation from the customer's point of view. Could it be that they gain that insight by asking better questions and listening more constructively? Of course. The top three criteria all revolve around the effective use of questions. A better question is the key to providing a deeper insight. There are questions, and then there are better questions.

Notice also that the advantage the superstars gain (seeing the situation from the customer's point of view) comes from excellent execution of a basic communications practice. They ask *better* questions.

I have a 3-year-old grandson. At that age, he can ask a question and listen to the answer. It is one of the very first communication devices a child learns. But my 3-year-old grandson can't ask a *better* question—he can't ask a question that is more effective than those voiced by the superstar salespeople. The point is this: Anyone can ask questions, but the best salespeople ask *better* questions.

If we are going to become *better* salespeople, we need to ask *better* questions.

Notice one other thing about the study. It did not say that superstar salespeople ask questions in a better *way*. Instead, it said that superstar salespeople ask *better questions*. The emphasis is on the question, not necessarily the manner or tone in which it is asked.

What, therefore, is a better question? It's a question such that its language does precisely what the salesperson wants it to do, and *only* what the salesperson wants it to do. The emphasis is on the *language* in the question. A better question is one in which the language is better.

For a salesperson, there is nothing more important than the language of the question. The language, as you know from the previous chapter, directs the customer's thinking. Ask the question one word off, and you'll direct the customer's thinking to places you may not necessarily want it to go.

Here's an example: When I first began my consulting business, one of the projects we would frequently encounter was that of creating and installing telemarketing programs with our clients. I had done just that with a client who was a seller of industrial scales. The telemarketer was focused on developing leads for the salespeople. A month or so after I had installed the program, I came back to visit with the client. Sitting across his desk from him I asked, "How's the telemarketing program going?"

He responded, "In one sense, it's going very well."

"How's that?" I replied.

"The telemarketer is developing more leads than we anticipated," he said.

"That's good," I replied.

"Not so good," he remarked.

"Oh?"

"Yes. I have a problem."

"What's your problem?"

"I can't get the salespeople to follow up on the leads."

"That is a problem," I remarked.

"So," he said, "I have a question."

"What's your question?" I asked.

"How do I get the salespeople to follow up on the leads?"

I thought for a moment and said, "I think that's the wrong question."

"What should I ask?"

"How do I get the leads followed-up on?"

Let's consider this exchange. When he asked the question, "How do I get the salespeople to follow up on the leads?" our thinking was going to be directed to "salespeople." Whatever solution we come up with will have to do with salespeople.

However, when we changed the language of the question to "How do I get the leads followed-up on?" it changed the focus of our thinking. Instead of focusing on the salespeople, we are now focused on the leads. And the range of creative solutions was dramatically expanded. For example, the solution *could* be something to do with the salespeople. But it could also involve independent reps, my client, the telemarketer, a fax/e-mail program, and so on. A simple change in the language of the question changed the course of our thinking and the solution that evolved. It was a *better* question.

Let's expand on this idea with some criteria for what constitutes a better sales question.

1. A better sales question takes account of the important variables: the customer, the depth of the relationship, and the purpose of the sales call.

A. The customer.

You would not necessarily ask the same question of an auto mechanic that you would of the CEO of a chain of 20 automotive repair facilities. So, the customer's position, the scope of her responsibility, and her educational level are factors to consider.

Probably even more important is the customer's communication style. I'm assuming that, at some point along the way, you have been exposed to the concept of different communication styles, and know that each person can be understood in terms of a category of communication style with which he or is most comfortable. Thus you would not ask the same question of a "director" that you would of an "influencer." For example, you wouldn't ask a director,

? How do you feel about that? ?

because he doesn't like to discuss feelings, and to ask that is to infringe on the customer's personal space. That question would be more appropriate for an influencer. A better question to the director would be,

? What do you think about that? ?

B. The depth of the relationship.

The deeper your relationship with the customer, the more unspoken permission you have to ask deeper questions. The reverse is also true: The shallower your relationship with the customer, the less unspoken permission you have to ask deep questions.

For example, you could not, in a first meeting with a new prospect, say something such as, "Tell me about your divorce!" You just don't have the permission to ask for information of that nature this early into the relationship.

On the other hand, the more personal history you have with the customer, the more unspoken permission you have to ask deeper and more penetrating questions. It takes a significant degree of trust and rapport for you to ask a question such as, "How do you really feel about your boss?"

In the hands of an effective salesperson, there is an interconnectedness between the depth and quality of the relationship you have with the customer and your ability to ask deeper questions. Not only does the relationship provide you permission to ask questions, but also the very act of asking ever deeper and more penetrating questions, by itself, deepens the relationship.

As you ask deeper questions, you cause the customer to think in ways in which he is not accustomed. And, as he shares his thoughts with you, the process of telling you things he doesn't tell other salespeople draws him closer to you, and you to him.

Often these kinds of questions go beyond the business level to the personal level. For example, questions such as the one following both assume a certain level of relationship, and help deepen the relationship:

? What do you, personally, really want to get out of this? ?

C. The purpose of the sales call.

At every stage of the sales process, you have a slightly different primary purpose for the sales call. The purpose of a sales call at the earlier stages of the sales process may be to collect information. Later, the purpose may be to propose your solution, or follow up on the implementation of a sale. Regardless, the language in your question is dependent upon the purpose of the sales call.

You would not ask a question such as, "What are you looking for?" if the purpose of the sales call is to close the deal. Nor would you ask a question such as, "Do you want one case or two?" if the purpose of the sales call is to uncover an opportunity.

Thus, the purpose of the sales call, and the place at which you are in the sales process, have a great deal to do with the language in your questions.

2. A better sales question should direct the customer's thinking appropriately.

This is, of course, the fundamental power of a question. As such, it should always be at the top of your mind. Sometimes you ask questions to gain information, and other questions you ask to influence the customer's thinking, regardless of your interest in the details of the answer. And sometimes the question is designed to do both. In either case, the language in your question influences the direction of your customer's thinking.

It is for this reason that you choose to use closed-ended or open-ended questions.

A closed-ended question is one that asks for a specific piece of information, and can be typically answered by one word—often a yes or no. For example, you could ask this closed-ended question:

? Is your business down this year? **?**

On the other hand, an open-ended question is one that calls for the customer to explain. It cannot be easily answered with one word. You could make this open-ended request:

? Tell me about how your business is doing this year. **?**

Neither one of these types of questions is always better than the other. The wise choice of one or the other is dependent on the situation. One is better than the other for the specifics of the sales call for which you are planning. For example, you may be making a first call on a prospect, and hoping to identify some opportunity for your products. An open-ended question is often a good way to begin, as it allows the customer the opportunity to direct the conversation to her needs before you are aware of them. It also flatters the customer, as it implies a sincere interest in her opinions, and a respect for her. A question such as the following would fit nicely:

? What are some of your highest-priority challenges? ?

On the other hand, in the same conversation with the customer, you may have identified an opportunity. Now is the time to narrow the customer's thinking down via a more closed-ended question such as,

? Is this important enough for you to devote a few minutes to explore some solutions? ?

As a general rule, salespeople are far too guilty of asking too many closed-ended questions, and not nearly enough open-ended questions.

3. A better sales question peels the onion.

The world is full of superficial salespeople who are content to ask superficial questions and address superficial problems with superficial solutions. It's the primary reason so many salespeople are fixated on price. One reason they find themselves talking about price, and responding to price questions and price objections, is that they have never taken the conversation to deeper levels. They have remained on the surface of the onion, afraid, unknowing, or unequipped to pursue deeper-in-the-onion issues.

Superficial questions are often a precursor to deeper questions, and are, therefore, necessary. A better salesperson, however, isn't content to focus on technical details, but peels the onion by inquiring into deeper issues.

For example, the typical salesperson asks questions such as these:

? What are you using? ?

? How many are you buying each month? ?

? From whom are you buying them? ?

These are all superficial questions that ask about the technical specifications of the deal. When you limit yourself to these kinds of questions, you limit your response to a presentation of your price.

The sales masters, however, dig deeper. They may ask those questions, but they don't stop there. They peel the onion by digging deeper:

? Why are you using that particular configuration? ?

? What is the impact of that on your process? ?

? What exactly are you trying to achieve with this component? ?

? To what degree would streamlining your process have a positive impact on the business? ?

? What do your customers think of this component? ?

These questions cause the customer to think about the issue in a deeper way, and they provide the salesperson with deeper, more significant information upon which to base a solution.

4. A better sales question takes into account the potential emotional effect of the question.

Every question has at least two aspects to it: The intellectual component and the emotional effect.

Although the primary function of a question is to address the intellectual piece (remember: a question directs the customer's thinking), an inappropriately phrased question can cause a negative emotional reaction in the customer.

For example, you could ask a question such as,

> What were you thinking when you made that stupid decision?

The intellectual component is appropriate—you want the customer to think about what was in his head at the time he made that decision. He probably will never get to the intellectual portion, however, because you have raised a powerful defensive emotional reaction with your poor choice of words. Emotions will trump the intellect.

Better sales questions, then, are based on a fundamental respect for the customer. He is a person of equal value to you, whose feelings need to be carefully considered, whose sensitivities need to be accounted for, and whose values need to be protected.

Better sales questions do not cause anyone—particularly your customer—to lose face. They can't imply blame or be negatively personal. So, something such as the following is probably not a good question:

> You sure blew that one, didn't you?

Finally, better sales questions are not manipulative. Manipulative questions violate the rule of respect for the customer by treating him or her as an object to be controlled. I lump into this category of manipulative questions those that many sales trainers advocate for "closing the sale," including the trial close.

Many customers will find a question such as the following to be highly manipulitave:

> **?** If I could save you 4 percent, is there any **?**
> reason why you would not buy this?

The customer knows she is being set up, and she resents you for doing that.

5. A better sales question does not seem capricious to the customer, or waste his or her time.

"Tell me about your business" used to be a good sales question. However, in today's information-rich world, it can be viewed as a time-waster by the customer. If you don't know about the business before you call on it, then you are wasting the customer's time. It may be a perfectly appropriate question from your point of view, but a time-waster from the customer's. The tremendous time pressures in our economy mean that customers are more defensive of their time than ever before.

In each of these categories lies fertile ground for mistakes in the language of your questions. Violate these criteria, and you'll find your customers irritated with you, and you'll be frustrated and unable to understand why you aren't selling to your potential. At the same time, these criteria can help you add power to your questions, energizing every stage of the sales process, and every interaction with your customers.

Preparation
Beats Inspiration

4 It may be that at some point in the distant future, you will become so adept at creating and asking better sales questions that you will just instinctively arrive at the very best choice of language on the spur of the moment. I wouldn't bet on it, though. All my experience tells me that the chances of you creating a series of better sales questions on the spur of the moment, when you are under the pressure of the moment, in the heat of the exchange with your customer, are dismal. If, however, you take the time to think about and then create those questions in the relatively relaxed time prior to the sales call, the likelihood is that your questions will be considerably more effective.

Which brings us to the first rule of asking better sales questions: Prepare your major questions, word-for-word, before the sales call.

This doesn't mean that you won't create questions during the sales call that seem appropriate in response to the customer's comments. Of course you will. But the major questions, the ones that provide the skeleton on which the sales call is built, should be created when you have the luxury of the time to think about them.

All my experience has taught me that preparation always trumps shoot-from-the-hip behavior. I recommend that you create three to five questions, word-for-word, for every important sales call.

In order to do so, take a few minutes prior to every sales call, and write down your responses to each step of the following process.

Step One: Describe the situation.

In a few words, describe the important details of the situation surrounding the sales call. Answer questions such as these:

? What type of account is this? **?**

? Where am I in the sales process? **?**

? Who is going to be on the other side? **?**

? What expectations do they have for this visit? **?**

There's no need for long, detailed descriptions—just a few bullets that capture the important elements of the situation in which you'll soon be entering.

Here's an example: I'm going to see, for the second time, the vice president of sales for one of my client companies. I've spoken with him a couple of times in the past, I know he has bought some of my training materials, and I suspect that he may be also considering a local trainer as an alternative. This time, the discussion is about an in-depth training program for all his salespeople.

In order to briefly capture all of that information, I'd note a few bullets:

- Client.
- Has some knowledge of me from the past.
- Looking at cheaper, local trainers.
- Wants an in-depth system.

Step Two: Describe your objectives.

? What do you want to achieve in this sales call? ?

? Why are you taking their time anyway? ?

Notice that these are self-questions—questions you ask yourself to sharpen and focus your thinking and the resulting behavior. A one-sentence response is a good way to consolidate your thinking and sharpen your focus.

In the last example, my purpose for the sales call is "To clearly and deeply understand his needs and interests as they relate to this particular issue."

Step Three: Brainstorm some sales questions.

Close your eyes and see yourself in the circumstances. Where are you? What is the customer doing? Now, create some sales questions and write them down, word-for-word. Remember, the words are important. Don't shortcut the process by summarizing—"I'll ask about this...." That leaves the creation of the exact words for the heat of the moment, and that is dangerous. Write your questions down, word-for-word, as you think of them.

This is one of the crucial steps in the process. It's here that you fold together all the elements of the situation and push them through the press of your objectives.

Let's start with the ultimate power of a good question: to influence and direct the customer's thinking. In this case, you are asking the question not so much to gain information, but to shape the customer's thinking.

Think of two basic directions in which you want to influence the customer's thinking—expanding and contracting her thinking. When you expand the customer's thinking, you prompt him to consider more than he has before. *More* could be more problems, more benefits, more issues, more reasons, more applications, and so on.

Contracting typically narrows the focus down to a specific issue. Expanding the customer's thinking comes, sequentially, before contracting.

Let's take one of my examples from a previous chapter— my discussion with my telemarketing program client. Remember, his question to me was,

? How do I get the salespeople to follow up on the leads? **?**

I prompted him to ask,

? How do I get the leads followed-up on? **?**

The first question contracted our thinking to one solution— the salespeople. When I prompted him to ask the broader question, it was an attempt to get him to think of more solutions before narrowing in on just one. By asking a broader question, we expanded the number of potential solutions. Then, when we had a number of possibilities identified, we could go on to selecting the best of those.

There is a powerful strategy here: First we expand, and then we contract. And we often go through this process several times, with each set of questions successively narrowing down more and more.

Follow this example: Let's start with my question:

? How do I get the leads followed-up on? ?

He could have said something similar to this: "Well, I suppose the telemarketer could do some of that. And some of the leads that look like they are for bigger deals could come right to me. And, with some of them, we could put in place a direct mail/e-mail program that would further qualify them."

He just expanded the number of potential solutions as a result of thinking of the answer to my question.

Now, let's contract with a question that asks him to prioritize:

? Which of those holds the greatest potential for immediate results? ?

He thinks for a moment and says, "The telemarketer. If we did that right, she could qualify some of them more precisely. That's what the salespeople complain about now."

We've gone from expanding to contracting. Now, we're going to go through the process again, this time focusing at a narrower perspective.

? How would you do that? ?

"We could create a more detailed qualifying form, and train the telemarketer to ask those questions of some of the leads. Of course, we'd have to create some criteria upon which ones to focus. And we'd have to script the call for her."

Now we're going to contract again.

? **What should you do first?** ?

"Create the criteria."

"Sounds good to me."

Let's consider what happened. My client, as many people—whether salespeople, managers, or customers—are so apt to do, jumped right from the problem to a knee-jerk solution. If he had gone on with his initial impulse to focus on the salespeople, he would have had a difficult, if not impossible, task in front of him: trying to change the behavior of a group of people who were set against him.

By encouraging him to expand, and then contract, and expand and then contract, he arrived at a course of action that would bring better results in the long run.

The expand/contract sequence is a powerful way to work with anyone: customers, managers, family, and friends.

Let's apply it to a typical selling situation. The first situation is a sequence of questions asked by a mediocre salesperson, and the second situation is managed by the sales master.

It's a first call on a prospect, and the widget salesperson is trying to uncover an opportunity that will provide him a reason to come back and make a second call. The customer is a purchasing agent.

<u>First Situation</u>

Salesperson: Do you use any widgets here?

P.A.: Some.

Salesperson: From whom do you buy them?

P.A.: We have a couple of different vendors.

Salesperson: How happy are you with your current suppliers?

P.A.: We're satisfied. We've been dealing with them for a long time.

Salesperson: Can I ask what you are paying for them?

P.A.: I'd rather not say.

Salesperson: Well, we provide exceptional customer service and our prices are generally below the competition.

P.A.: Hmmm.

Salesperson: Can I quote you on our price?

P.A.: Sure. Send me an e-mail.

Salesperson: Okay.

P.A.: I have to go now.

Second Situation

Salesperson: What are some of the categories of product for which you are responsible?

P.A.: I buy widgets, gidgets, and pidgets.

Salesperson: Sounds like a lot of responsibility. What are some of the issues with which you are dealing these days in regard to your widgets?

P.A.: We are generally content. But..well, we do have some issues with quality.

Salesperson: Quality. I see. Anything else?

P.A.: That's the big issue.

Salesperson: If you have a quality problem, where does that impact you the most—in the production process, or increasing your costs, or jeopardizing your relationship with your customers?

P.A.: Actually, all of the above.

Salesperson: Sounds like a problem.

P.A.: Yep.

Salesperson: You know, we've dealt with these issues successfully with other companies similar to yours. You may have heard of Smith Brothers, or Jones Manufacturing?

P.A.: I've heard of Jones.

Salesperson: Good. How about if we get together next week, and I share some ideas that were able to help Jones and others like you make widget quality issues a thing of the past? I'll need about 30 minutes.

P.A.: Okay.

Salesperson: I've got time on Wednesday afternoon or Thursday morning. Which is better?

P.A.: Wednesday.

The mediocre salesperson asked routine, superficial questions, got routine, superficial answers, and defaulted to price. The sales master got the customer thinking of things that were important to her, then influenced her to consider the gravity of those issues, hinted at a solution, and used that to secure the second appointment. That's how it is done. The power is in the question.

Much of the rest of the book focuses on helping you develop better questions for all of your selling situations.

Let me refer back to the example of selling my services to an existing client. I'll brainstorm some questions. I could ask:

? What is your budget? ?

? What sort of solution are you looking for? ?

? Who is going to make this decision? ?

? What exactly are you looking for? ?

? When do you want to do this? ?

? How many salespeople will be involved? ?

? Will you want to train future salespeople in this process? ?

? How important is it that you have a reproducible system? ?

? What do you see as the potential impact on the company? ?

Step Four: Edit your questions.

At this point, you will have created a long list of questions—maybe 10 or so. You've been creative. Now it's time to become critical. Look at your list of questions and methodically apply the criteria we discussed in the previous chapter.

Here are the criteria:

1. A better sales question takes account of the important variables: the customer, the depth of the relationship, and the purpose of the sales call.
2. A better sales question should direct the customer's thinking appropriately.
3. A better sales question peels the onion.
4. A better sales question takes account of the potential emotional effect of the question.
5. A better sales question does not seem capricious to the customer, nor waste his or her time.

Look at each question, and ask these questions about it:

1. Is this question shaped for the uniqueness of this particular customer?

2. Is this question appropriate for the depth of the relationship I have with this customer?

3. Does this question move me closer to obtaining my objective?

4. If the customer thinks of the answer to my question, is that what I want him to think?

5. Does this question get at issues that are deeper than the most superficial?

6. Is there anything in the language of this question that might have a negative emotional effect on the customer?

It is not necessary that every question meet the criteria 100 percent. For example, you could look at your question and say no to criteria number 1, because this is the first time you have met this customer, and don't know anything about her. Or, you could realize that your question is very superficial, and doesn't meet the third criteria. But you must ask some superficial questions to begin the conversation and get the customer in an information-giving mode before you dig deeper. So, under the circumstances, it's okay that this particular question doesn't meet that criterion.

The real purpose of this part of the process is to get you to think, from the customer's point of view, about the language in your question. Just this process of considering the language will cause you to make changes in many of the questions. And that alone will improve your questions, and, therefore, improve your results.

Whenever you consider a question and realize, by applying these criteria, that it isn't as good as it could be, rephrase the question. Try it again with different language. Could you use an open-ended version? Could you try to expand or contract the customer's thinking? Could you eliminate those words that may be offensive?

Eventually, you'll arrive at a new set of questions that are much better than those with which you started.

Let's apply this process to the questions I created at the end of the previous section. Here they are again:

? What is your budget? ?

? What sort of solution are you looking for? ?

? Who is going to make this decision? ?

? What exactly are you looking for? ?

? When do you want to do this? ?

? How many salespeople will be involved? ?

? Will you want to train future salespeople in this process? ?

? How important is it that you have a reproducible system? ?

? What is the potential effect on the company? ?

As I look at all of these questions, I'm struck with the fact that they seem a bit too blunt and to the point. My contact is much more of a people person, and these questions need to be softened a bit. (Criterion number 1.)

It also occurs to me that I haven't really directed the customer's thinking to anything that would provide me an advantage in the sales competition. I need to peel the onion, and uncover some substantial issues upon which I can build. (Criterion number 2.)

With those two realizations, I start to work rewriting the questions. I'll start out, I decide, with a couple of pure information-type (technical specification) questions.

? How many salespeople will be involved? ?

? When do you want to do this? ?

Now, I want to start digging a little deeper. I come up with this:

? When the training is all done, what do you want the sales force to look like? How will they be different? ?

What he really wants is not training, I reason, but the result of training. Let's dig to that level.

Which brings me to another deep-in-the-onion question:

? You've been here a few years, and training the salespeople is only now at the top of your priority list. Why is that? What's changed? ?

As long as I'm at it, let's cut to the heart of the matter:

? How will the success of this program, or the lack of it, affect you personally? ?

With some frank responses to these questions, I should have sufficient material on which to build my proposal. I decide to use a couple more questions. Instead of the budget question, I'm going to be softer:

? What is the range of the investment **?**
you anticipate making?

And then, finally:

? Who, besides you, will be involved **?**
in making the decision?

I now have a far more effective set of questions. It's taken me about 10 minutes to work through this process. Ten minutes well spent.

Step Five: Capture them.

You should have, at this point, a revised set of three to six questions with which you are happy. Now, write them down in the format that is most comfortable for you. How do you organize yourself in a sales call? Do you use a yellow pad, a PDA, a day timer, or a laptop? Put your questions into your preferred organizational tool, so they are ready for you to refer to when the time comes.

In my days of full-time selling, I would write them on 3 × 5 cards, which was my organizational tool. I'd store them in my breast-pocket wallet, and take them out and stick them into the top of a yellow pad on which I took notes. They were always available when I needed to refer to them.

In a 10-week sales training program, I gave everyone the assignment to prepare to ask better questions. At the beginning of the next session, I asked each student to share with the class how he or she had completed the assignment. One student stood up and held up a three-ring binder. In the inside back cover of the binder was a yellow pad on which to take notes. The rings of the binder contained several plastic inserts—the kind that allows you to slide a piece of paper inside and then attach the plastic sheet through the three holes. Each plastic sheet contained a page with a description of the type of sales call on the top, and several questions, written in a large, easy-to-read font, on the page. He would take the plastic sheet that contained the questions for the sales call out and position it on top of the others prior to each sales call.

It was perfect! I remarked to the class that it was an example of a professional salesperson methodically preparing to make use of his most powerful sales tool.

Step Six: Practice!

You don't need to memorize your questions, but you do need to make sure that you can pronounce the words accurately, and that you can ask the question in an appropriate tone of voice for the customer and the situation.

So take a moment and practice them. A few moments of preparation can make a big difference in implementation.

A word about collecting better questions

After you go through this process a few times, you'll discover that you are using some questions, or portions of questions, over and over. You will have rendered your hard work into some extremely useful questions.

Save them. Begin to classify them. Think of the sales process: better questions for a cold call, better questions for uncovering the customer's concerns, better closing questions, and so on. Think of the kind of customer: better questions for a purchasing agent, better questions for a CFO, better questions for a shop foreman, and so on.

I believe a better question is a powerful tool, and as you uncover and collect better questions, you add tools to your toolbox. Just the way an experienced tradesman, say an electrician or carpenter, is expected to have a truck full of the right tools for the right situations, so too are you. That comes with time.

Not only will you add the questions that you develop to your toolbox, but this process of considering the language of your questions and analyzing the language in them will also make you much more sensitive to the questions you hear around you. Whenever you hear a better question, capture it. Write it down. Try it out. If it fits, add it to your toolbox.

A year from now, you'll be far better equipped with powerful tools than you are today. And a few years from now, you will be a force with which to be reckoned.

As we go through each of the chapters of this book, you'll see some excellent sales questions. Write them down, put them into your toolbox, and discipline yourself to use them appropriately. Here is one such better, all-purpose question to begin your tool collection:

? Anything else? ?

This is one of my favorite questions. It shows you are listening to the customer and are interested in her opinions. It can be used in an unlimited number of sales situations, and it can be used over and over. It always peels the onion, by asking for more (and usually deeper) information.

Here's an example of how to use it. Let's say you asked one of the questions from my example, such as,

? When the training is all done, what do you want the sales force to look like? How will they be different? ?

The customer thinks for a moment before answering: "We really want to have a professional sales force, one that can take a product and create a market for it. They would be capable of routinely doing that."

I reply,

? A sales force like that would be a ?
   powerful asset. Anything else?

"You know, we don't make anything here, we just sell products that other companies make. Our ability to create a market for new products will allow us to continually be the first choice of vendors looking for a way to market their products."

? So you really see this as a long-term strategic asset ?
      for the company. Anything else?

"I want a sales force of which I can personally be proud. I want that to be my legacy in this company."

"Got it."

At this point, I think I have uncovered some deep motivations on which I can build.

Questioning
Combinations and
Techniques

5

Hopefully, as a result of reading this book, you will have gained a rich and practical understanding of the importance of the language in your questions, and a work- ing knowledge of how to create a better sales question. And, although that is of ut- most importance, it's not the only aspect of asking ques- tions you can take to a higher level. Once you understand the process of creating better sales questions, the issue is to string two or more questions together in effective combinations, and then to use some tactical questioning techniques for spur-of-the moment situations.

Let's start with some traditional, multipurpose com- binations of questions.

Superficial – Personal

This is a natural ordering of your questions based on the subject of the question. It's a reflection of the fact that it takes a little time and conversation to make someone comfortable enough with you for them to share anything of significance with you.

So, for example, you start out with superficial questions:

? How about those Yankees? ?

? Sure is hot, isn't it? ?

After having generated some superficial conversation, your customer is feeling comfortable enough for you to probe into the business issues.

? How is this process working for you? ?

? What is it that you are trying to accomplish here? ?

Now the customer is sharing important business information. Many salespeople stop here. But the masters often take the discovery process one layer deeper by probing into the implications on the individual decision-makers. In other words, they uncover how the deal affects the people. These questions are best asked, sequentially, after the first two types. It takes the development of a sense of trust for the customer to feel comfortable enough to answer these kinds of questions with any accuracy.

? What are some of the challenges you ? personally are facing in the job?

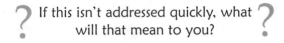

In this case, you began the sales call with the purpose of uncovering the information revealed in the third set of questions. However, you understood that you had to go through the superficial-business-personal sequence in order to get there.

The funnel

Probably the most useful questioning sequence is called the funnel. Picture a funnel, open wide at the top and gradually narrowing down to a much smaller opening at the bottom. (See Illustration 2.)

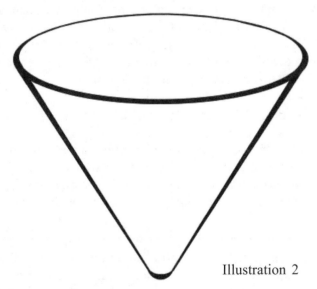

Illustration 2

That's a great graphic image of the strategy behind the funnel technique. Your focus and the breadth of the information you request of the customer is wide open at first, and then gradually narrows down to a specific piece of information at the end of the sequence.

Let's work through an example. Let's say you are selling software, and you have a menu of programs for various business applications.

So you start out with a broad, open-ended question or request to prompt a broad response from the customer; something such as,

? Tell me about the challenges you are facing right now. ?

The customer explains that the company has a goal of growing by 10 percent this year, and that puts pressure on everyone. In addition, he's having some problems with turnover in his department—it's so difficult to find good people these days.

You could choose to try to get the customer to expand by asking the question "Anything else?" at this point, but you're happy that he has expressed the goal of growing by 10 percent—that's something with which you can work. So you focus on that, and narrow your question down a bit.

? How does that growth goal of 10 percent affect you? ?

Notice that the focus of the question is narrower than the first question, and that the subject about which you are inquiring is one that came out of the customer's first answer. You are in the funnel now, narrowing the customer's thinking from broad to specific.

The customer answers, "We have to come up with a plan to handle 10 percent more information and transactions flowing through this department. They don't want us to add any employees, and we've got this issue of replacing those who leave."

You respond,

? So, it sounds as though the real problem is productivity—how to get more production out of the people you have. Is that right? ?

The customer thinks for a moment and says, "Yes. That would be the solution. We have to get more production out of each employee."

That, now, is an open door for you to walk through and begin to explain the benefits of some of your software in terms of increased productivity. Your product is a solution to the customer's problem. The way you uncovered the customer's problem was by using the funnel approach—starting with a broad, open-ended question, and then narrowing the customer's thinking down until you arrived at a specific issue.

The bagpipe

Imagine a bagpipe—the musical instrument played by filling a bladder with air, and then squeezing the air out in narrow tubes. The air bladder is first expanded, and then contracted. That's a great image for a fundamental questioning technique that can be used in countless situations. First you expand the breadth of the customer's thinking and resultant responses by asking one or two broad, open-ended questions. For example, let's say you are selling for me—sales training. You start out by attempting to broaden the customer's thinking and cover a wide range of possibilities with a question such as,

? What are your feelings about the state of your sales force? ?

Or,

? What are some of your concerns about the
state of your sales force? ?

The customer responds by mentioning that the economy is changing rapidly, and he is not so sure his sales force is keeping up. He has a number of salespeople who have become content and complacent. And he's not quite sure of his company's ability to attract new and motivated salespeople.

Your job now is to contract his thinking to one or two issues into which you want to probe. You'd like to understand
the customer's top issue. So, you say something similar to this:

> Which of those, if you could solve it, would make the
> biggest effect on the company's sales?

The customer thinks for a minute and replies, "If I could
shake up some of the content salespeople and get them motivated, I think I'd see an immediate improvement in sales."

You've contracted his thinking down to one issue. Think
bagpipe. You can now continue this process of expanding and
contracting a multiple number of times. Let's take it one layer
deeper. We now know which issue is the highest priority for
the customer. Let's expand and contract that issue.

> I'm sure you've thought about that. What are
> some of the ideas you've come up with?

That question expands the customer's thinking.

He says, "Well, I've thought of changing the compensation plan, of firing one as a message to the others, and of providing them some training so that they know how to sell more
effectively in this economy."

Let's now contract his thinking to one issue:

> Of those, which do you think is the one which will most
> likely improve the productivity of most of them?

He thinks for a minute and says, "I'm a little unsure about
compensation, and firing one may just backfire on me. Probably training."

We're having fun here, so let's expand and contract one
more time.

? What do you see as the benefits of training them? ?

"Well, they would know how to do their jobs better. I don't think they have ever been trained in how to do sales well. And that confidence would spill over and help motivate them to actually improve themselves and their performance."

? So, it sounds as though training may be the single most effective solution to your sales force concerns. Is that right? ?

"Yes."

Expand, contract. Expand, contract. Just like a bagpipe.

The list

Use the "list" as a technique to gain an understanding of the customer and a glimpse of the customer's values. This technique is best used with a customer who isn't talkative. You've tried open-ended questions and discovered that the customer responds in a protective, non-disclosing sort of way. You are unable to gain any significant information because the customer just doesn't respond well to open-ended questions.

So, you fall back to plan B—using the list. This technique is just what it sounds like: You have a list of items, and you ask the customer to select from it. Depending on where you are in the sales process and what specific information you are trying to uncover, the selection can be which of them is most important to him, which is the highest of his concerns, which most accurately describes his position, and so on.

For example, you may be working with the price objection— the customer has indicated that your price is too high. So now you want to find out what exactly he means by that. You decide to use the list technique. So you say this:

"Thanks, John, I appreciate you sharing that with me. Can you help me to understand exactly what you mean by that?

When you say that our price is too high, which of these four statements best describes exactly what you mean?

1. You can't afford it.
2. It's more than you thought it would be.
3. It's more than it's worth.
4. You can get something similar, cheaper."

Question the answer

Here's another combination that has lots of applications. I call it "question the answer." You use it in a situation in which you want to dig deeper with a customer in order to uncover the deepest issues you can. The technique is simple—you just question the customer's answer.

Here's an example: Let's say that you made a major proposal two weeks ago, and you haven't heard anything. You are back in front of the customer now, with the purpose of trying to ascertain where you stand, so that you have the opportunity to negotiate the deal. You begin with a straightforward, open-ended question:

> **?** How are we looking on that proposal? **?**

The customer thinks for a moment and then replies, "Not bad, really."

Not content to accept that superficial response, you then question the answer.

> **?** Okay. Help me understand. When you say "not bad," what exactly does that mean? **?**

The customer says, "Well, we liked the breadth of your proposal, and, honestly, we thought the pricing was fair."

You ask:

Anything else?

The customer responds, "Yes, there were a few other things."

You again question the answer:

What other things?

"There was some concern about your ability to deliver."

Now we're talking, but you still haven't gotten to the heart of the issue. One more time, you question the answer.

Oh?

"Yes. We know that you deliver to this area only once a week, and we'll need more frequent delivery if we are going to do this."

Now you've uncovered the issue. You can determine what to do with this information. Prior to having that option, you first had to uncover it. Questioning the answer was the combination of questions that helped you uncover the information you needed.

Buffering

Here's a technique to use when you want to ask a question that you know may be awkward or difficult for the customer to answer. For example, you want to ask the customer,

 Is your business down this year?

You know that he's quite proud of her business, and admitting that it is not doing so well this year will be difficult for her. You want to spare her that awkwardness, and assure yourself of getting an accurate and honest answer. So you decide to buffer the question.

Think of a buffered aspirin: It softens the impact of the aspirin, making it more tolerable. That's the idea. You want to soften the impact of your question, making it more tolerable for the customer to answer.

There are two ways to do this. First, tell a story about some other people, and then ask if he is like the people in the story. So you say something similar to this:

> **?** Several of my customers are experiencing a slowdown in business due to the economy and the softening of the market. I wonder, is your business is like theirs? **?**

It's easier for the customer to answer that question, because you have buffered it for her. Here's the second way to buffer a question: Make a factual statement. Make an observation. Ask the question. Here are some examples:

> **?** The market is shrinking and a lot of companies are cutting back. It must be really difficult to operate in this market. Your business is probably down a bit as well, isn't it? **?**

You can, of course, buffer any question by making the language a bit more abstract. For example, instead of saying,

> **?** Is your business down this year? **?**

You could say,

> **?** Is the economy negatively affecting your revenues this year? **?**

"Negatively affecting your revenues," is much more abstract than "down," and so is easier to answer.

Notice another technique: It's easier to answer a question about someone else, or something else, than about you. So, in the second question, you asked about the economy; in the first, "your business" was the subject of the question.

All-purpose questions

Some questions are so handy that coupling them with another question to form a sequence can become almost second nature. You use them in almost every conversation.

I love the question "Oh?" for example. We've already discussed the all-purpose question, "Anything else?" used to follow up on almost any question. You may ask, for example, the question,

? Is the economy negatively affecting
your revenues this year? ?

The customer may say something such as, "Well, yeah—to a certain degree. Our x-product sales are down a bit from last year." You say, "Oh?" He says, "That new product line we had high hopes for has tanked." You say, "Anything else?" He says, "We've had to lay three people off in production."

Because you sell production equipment, you have finally gotten the piece of information you wanted. It took one good buffered question, an "Anything else?" and an "Oh?" to get there.

When you ask "Oh?" follow it with silence. Just be quiet until the customer talks.

You may be afraid of what you perceive to be a moment of awkward silence. But the customer rarely perceives it that way. She is thinking about what she is going to say.

"Oh?" because it is more open, can lead to subjects you didn't know existed, whereas "anything else?" directs the customer to think about the content in his last answer. For example, when you asked the question, "Is the economy negatively affecting your revenues this year?" the customer could have answered the same way: "Well, yeah. To a certain degree. Our x-product sales are down a bit from last year." You say, "Oh?" The customer pauses for a minute and then says, "Those miserable SOBs in Congress. They just sit on their behinds and fool with the economy. We ought to throw them all out." That didn't really further your cause, but it did you give an insight into his political beliefs. You'll know where not to go in subsequent conversations.

Although "Oh?" can lead you down unexpected paths, it is a powerful question you should put into your toolbox. In one training session, I gave everyone the assignment to ask the question "Oh?" at least 10 times in the next week. One of the participants couldn't wait to report on her experience. She sold for a substance abuse treatment facility, and called on companies in an attempt to get them to add her facility as one of their benefits. She reported that several projects had been stuck and just not moving. When she asked the question "Oh?" repeatedly, the customers thought and talked themselves into a more proactive course, and she revived a couple of stuck projects.

───────

Are you gaining an appreciation for just how rich the world of sales questions is? We have just begun the process of understanding the power of a better sales question, and some techniques to apply those questions. In the rest of the book, we'll apply these ideas to a selection of sales situations, and review questions created by real salespeople in my seminars.

Focusing on the Essential Steps in the Sales Process

6 I like to keep things simple. I recall one of my clients showing me the flow-chart of his sales process: 26 steps. That level of detail may have been appropriate for that specific situation, but it's overkill when we are talking about the application for a typical professional salesperson.

The job of the salesperson is much like playing golf. In a four-hour round of golf, the club hitting the ball only takes about three minutes; everything else is prelude or postlude. The essence of the game is, of course, to hit the ball correctly.

The same thing is true of sales. The essence is to interact with the customer effectively. Everything else is prelude or postlude. The best golfers execute the essentials with excellence. They focus on the three minutes. The best salespeople execute the essentials with excellence. They focus on the quantity and quality of their interactions with their customers.

So, regardless of the intricacies of the customer, the product, and the setting, the job of the salesperson can be reduced to these basic elements:

1. Engage with the right people.
2. Make them feel comfortable with you.
3. Find out what they want.
4. Show them how what you have provides them what they want.
5. Gain agreement on the next step.
6. Ensure that they are satisfied, and leverage that satisfaction to other opportunities.

Let's examine each step in this simple sales process.

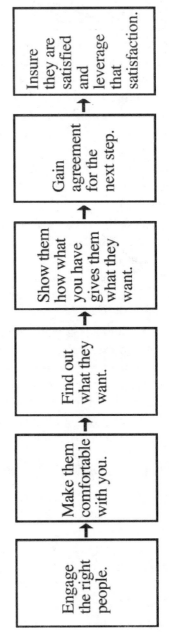

Illustration 3

1. Engage with the right people.

You can be the most trained, thoroughly equipped sales-person in the world, with the best questions, the most powerful presentation, and the gift of a good sense of humor, but if you waste all this on the wrong people, you'll never be successful.

Engaging with the right people is absolutely essential. However, it is far more difficult today than ever before. And it is growing more difficult, as more of your customers find themselves in overstressed situations in which they have too much to do and not enough time to do it. That puts meeting with you at the bottom of their to-do lists.

In order to be successful at this, you must identify all the key people, prioritize them, and then develop a series of practices that will allow you to regularly gain an audience with them. No small task. In fact, you'll need to work at this, constantly improving, for the rest of your career. It's that big of a challenge.

A good series of questions is a major tool to help you do this. They will provide you with the information that enables you to identify the important people to see, and allow you to collect and then prioritize the potential in every opportunity. A good series of questions, asked about the customer, will provide you with the information you need to sculpt your approach and turn the first encounter into a full-scale engagement.

2. Make your customers feel comfortable with you.

If they aren't comfortable with you, they won't spend much time with you, and the time that they do spend will be guarded and tentative. They may be convinced to do business with you because of the fundamental attractiveness of your offer, but it will be action taken against the grain. They will be forever uncomfortable and eager to find a replacement.

On the other hand, if they are comfortable with you, they won't mind spending time with you. They'll be much more open to sharing the information that is necessary for you to do a good job of crafting a solution. They'll be eager to share future opportunities with you and will be much easier to deal with.

Using a series of perceptive questions develops the perception of your competence within the customer, leading him to sense that you are competent and trustworthy. A series of personal questions leads the customer to perceive that you are interested in him, a necessary step to him feeling comfortable with you. A series of good questions uncovers areas you and your customer may have in common—another important aspect of creating a feeling of comfort.

Without the use of good questions, you are powerless to make a customer feel comfortable with you.

3. Find out what they want.

I believe this step is the heart of selling—the essence of what a salesperson is all about. I know that flies in the face of the routine practices of multitudes of salespeople who believe that the end all of their focus is to push their product. It is certainly true that the company expects you to sell your product, but the issue is how you sell it.

You can proclaim the merits of your product to willing and unwilling listeners far and wide, attempting to sway them with the powerful features and advantages your product offers over the competition. Or you can focus on the customer, finding out what motivates him, what issues are important to him, what problems he has, what objectives he is trying to achieve, what he looks for in a vendor, and so on.

I call the sum total of the customer's needs the *gap*. Having fully understood the gap—or "what he wants"—you can then present your product as a means of filling that vacuum, of giving him what he wants.

This is true tactically, in an immediate sense, during a specific sales call, as well as strategically, in time and a series of

sales calls. For example, if you ask the customer for an appointment, and in so doing mention a question that the customer may have, or a problem that the customer may be
experiencing that you can solve, and if your assumption is accurate, then your request for the customer's time will be far
more effective than if you just talk about your product. I remember one somewhat defensive salesperson telling me at one
of my seminars that he "just tells them that I want to talk to
them about my company and my products." Needless to say,
his approach wasn't very effective.

It would be far more effective to say something such as:
"Because you are this kind of company, I believe you have this
issue, and we can help you with that." The conversation here is
about what the customer wants, not your product.

Strategically, the same is true. You may make five or six
sales calls on a nice-sized account, specifically for the purpose
of discovering, in depth and detail, what the customer wants.
Everything that comes before is designed to get to this understanding, and everything you do after is based on this step. It is
the fulcrum upon which the entire sales process pivots.

The primary way you learn, with depth and detail, what the
customer wants, is to ask good questions.

4. Show them how what you have gives them what they want.

Sooner or later you have to make an offer to your customers.
In order for you to sell anything, they must decide to buy it. And
if they are going to buy it, you need to make them aware of it.

You can go about your territory, loudly proclaiming the
features of your product to whomever will listen. Or you can
craft your offer in such a way as to begin with what they want,
and show them how your offer gives them what they want.

Proclaiming your product's features is the preferred routine of the mediocre salesperson. Personally and individually

crafting your presentation to show the customer how what you have gives him what he wants is the mindset that, in part, defines the master salespeople.

But a presentation isn't a static thing. The best salespeople finely tune their presentations to the signals they receive from the customer, making mid-term—and in some cases, mid-sentence—changes to reflect their perceptions of how the customer is receiving their communications.

Thus, a series of well-planned, appropriately placed questions spread throughout the presentation is an effective way to add power to your presentations.

5. Gain agreement on the next step.

Every sales interaction has an assumed next step. If you call someone for an appointment, the next step is the appointment. If you present your solution to a decision-maker, the next step is the order. In between, there are thousands of potentially different sales calls, and thousands of potential action steps that follow the sales call.

The agreement is the ultimate rationale for the sales call, and the aspect that makes it a "sales" call. If you aren't expecting to gain any agreement, then why are you making the call? It's not a sales call. It may be a public relations call, or a something-to-do call, but it's not a sales call. A sales call is set apart from the rest of the interactions in this world by the fact that it anticipates an agreement.

Without an agreement, the process has been a waste of time. It is the ultimate goal of every salesperson, and of every sales process, and of every sales call.

Clearly, you generally don't gain agreement without asking for it. There's that question again.

6. Ensure that they are satisfied, and leverage that satisfaction to uncover other opportunities.

This is the one step in the sales process that is most commonly neglected. Most salespeople are so focused on making the sale that they neglect to consider that their real purpose is to satisfy the customer. And that extends beyond just the sale itself.

The sales call on the customer, made after the sale is complete, delivered, and implemented by the customer, is one of the most powerful sales calls available. In it, the salesperson seeks assurance that the customer is satisfied, and then leverages that affirmation to uncover additional opportunities with the customer and/or referrals to people in other organizations.

And, clearly, how would you find out if the customer is satisfied, without asking? And how would you uncover additional opportunities, other than to ask? How would you gain referrals, if you did not ask? Questions, once again, are the key tool to this and every step in the sales process.

Taking it to another level

I have just presented six simple steps to the sales process, applicable to almost every sales situation. Ah, if only it were that simple. It doesn't take a genius to realize that, though the list may be simple, the job of accomplishing each step with sufficient quantity and quality is a lifetime challenge. Each of these simple steps is really an incredibly complex compendium of hundreds of sub-processes, paradigms, and practices.

A salesperson devoted to continually improving his or her results should focus on doing each of these ever better for the rest of his or her career. Let's look at each of these in a bit more detail. I said earlier that all sales can be reduced to these simple steps. Let's test that theory by examining several scenarios.

Here's one: You are calling a prospect to make an appointment to see her. She doesn't know you. Amazingly, she answers her phone, and you now have about 30 seconds to get her into a conversation, the result of which you hope to be an agreement for an appointment. We've already included the "right person" portion of the process. In the next 30 seconds or so, your job is to:

1. Make her comfortable with you.
2. Find out what she wants, at a very superficial level.
3. Show her how an appointment with you will help give her what she wants.
4. Gain her agreement to meet with you.

If you can do that, you'll gain the appointment (the agreement), which is why you called in the first place. In this case, you've attempted to work through four steps in a matter of seconds.

Let's look at the opposite side of the spectrum with a long-term, strategic application of this system. You are selling capital equipment, with an 18-month selling cycle. Your process looks something similar to this:

1. You first call the account to introduce yourself and qualify the account. You discover that the account is qualified, so you attempt to discover the names of the key decision-makers. (Step One: Engage with the key people. You must first identify the key people before you can engage with them.)

2. You call for an appointment. It takes several phone attempts, but finally you get to one of the key people, the assistant plant manager, and he agrees to see you. (You are still at step one.)

3. You now make the first live sales call to a key person. Your job is to gain a second appointment. In this first call, you:

    a.   Make him comfortable with you.

    b.   Get a sense of some of his issues (find out what he wants).

    c.   Suggest that you may be able to help with those, and that a longer, more intense information-collecting visit would be in order (show how what you have gives them what they want).

    d.   Gain an agreement for the next appointment.

4. At the next live visit with the assistant plant manager:

    a.   You continue to work on making him comfortable with you.

    b.   You ask specific questions to dig deeper into his issues and challenges (finding out what he wants).

    c.   It becomes clear that you'll need to have this same discussion with the production foreman as well as the chief financial officer. So you suggest that, in order for you to craft a solution that will appeal to them, you'll need to collect some additional information from these two people (show him how what you have gives him what he wants).

    d.   You ask him to set up appointments for you to see each of these two people. He agrees (get an agreement for the next step).

5. You attain visits with each of the remaining key people: the production foreman and the chief financial officer. You know by now what you do in each of these visits. You:

a.   Make them comfortable with you.

b.   Find out what they want.

c.   Suggest that you create a proposal (creating some anticipation in them for you to show them how what you have gives them what they want).

d.   Get an agreement for the next step—a proposal and presentation to the three key people, assembled together (agreement on the next step).

Notice that, on a strategic scale, you are still at the "find out what they want" step. However, tactically, you did that in each of the sales calls.

If we were to continue this explication of the sales process, you'd see the five steps developing throughout the length of the sales process, and also occurring at each visit. Processes within processes.

On the following page is a graphic way to view this.

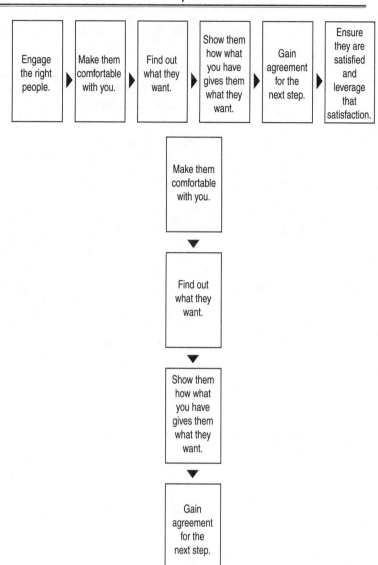

Illustration 4

As you can see, becoming more effective at every step in the sales process is the path to career-long growth. And, because questions are the essential tool to accomplish each step with excellence, by focusing on mastering the art of asking questions, you focus your efforts on the one place that will bring the greatest results.

Questions to Help You Engage the Right People

7 Engaging the right people is the essential first step in the sales process. That means entering into a personal dialogue with people who can make or influence the decision. You gather some information about their situations, and you share some information about your company and its products and services. You can engage with them over the phone or in person.

Notice that there are two aspects to this step in the process. First, you must identify the right people, and then you must get into a conversation with them.

Some salespeople are too timid to make sure that the person who sees them is the person to whom they should be talking. Others are afraid of rejection, and so limit their energies to those with whom they are comfortable. Neither of these two common errors are effective sales practices. If you are going to be effective, you must spend most of your time with those prospects and customers who are closest to the decision.

In my book *10 Secrets of Time Management for Salespeople*, I discuss the concept of "effective" sales practices. The concept is this: Salespeople have so much to do in the course of the average work week, they can't possibly do everything that presents itself. Rather than try to jam more and more tasks into the course of their day, they are much better served by focusing on the most effective, highest-potential items, and give them priority.

One way to do that is to consider the concept of *sales time*. *Sales time* refers to that portion of the work week when you are actually engaged in conversation with your prospects and customers. In most sales territories, that is roughly 10 to 14 hours per week.

One of the keys to becoming highly effective is to focus on investing your limited sales time where it will bring you the best return for it. Think of this analogy: Let's say you have some money in a retirement account. You can make certain observations about that. For one, you know that the money is measurable. You can determine, at any one moment in time, exactly how much there is. Secondly, you know it is limited. It is not an unlimited supply, and you would be hard pressed to double it tomorrow. Finally, you know that, to the extent that you have the ability to dictate where it is invested, the decisions you make about the investment of that money will determine your standard of living at some point in the future. If you make wise decisions about the investment of your money, you may be able to take that trip to Europe, or the major cruise of which you have been dreaming. If you don't make good decisions about the investment of your money, you won't be able to do those things. So your decisions about how you invest your money will directly affect your standard of living.

Now, consider your sales time. What do you know about it? First, that it, like your money, is measurable. If I was to follow you around last week with a stop watch in my hand, I'd have been able to measure exactly how much time you spent interacting with your prospects and customers. Second, you know that it is a limited amount. You would be hard pressed to double it next week. Finally, you know that the decisions you make about the investment of your sales time will affect your standard of living. Make wise decisions, and you earn more incentives and commissions, and are able to live better and provide more for your families. Make poor decisions, and you won't have the additional income to improve your standard of living. Your time is just like your money—an income-producing asset you must invest with wise and thoughtful decisions. Which brings us to the following processes. The mediocre salesperson is happy to have anyone upon whom to call. The top-performing salespeople make wise decisions about in whom they invest their selling time.

In order to do that, you must methodically execute three different practices:

1. You must identify a tentative list of people.
2. You must qualify them, so that you know they are the right people.
3. You must engage with them.

Let's look at how you can use questions to effectively accomplish each of these three steps.

1. Identify a tentative list of people.

You must start somewhere. The place to start is with a list of "suspects." Suspects are people—potential customers—whom you suspect may be prospects. At this point, they are suspects because you know little about them, and don't know for sure that they are high-potential "prospects." Prospects are people who have a legitimate need for what you sell, can make or influence the decision, and who can pay for it. The process of turning a suspect into a prospect is called "qualifying," and that is step two.

For now, let's focus on the first step. How do you identify a tentative list? In some selling situations, this is already done for you by your company. For example, you may receive a steady stream of leads from your company's marketing efforts. Those leads are suspects. As you accumulate them, you gradually develop a list of suspects.

In other selling situations, you must develop your own list. The best way to do this is to create a profile of your best customers, and then to apply that profile to the world at large and see who most closely resembles your best customers. Those then become your highest-potential suspects.

This is a place where the questions you ask yourself are of highest importance. Begin by creating a list of questions you ask yourself about your customer base. Here are some typical questions:

? In what market segments are my best customers? ?

? What size are they, as determined by number of ?
employees, or some other measurement?

? Does their location have anything ?
to do with it? If so, what?

? Do they have any particular organizational ?
structure that sets them apart?

? Do they use any specific equipment, sell to any specific ?
markets, or have any other identifiable characteristics?

? What other demographics best ?
describe my best customers?

When you have answered these questions, you put the answers together into a profile, and then use that profile to identify high-potential suspects. For example, let's say you have created a profile that looks something similar to this:

- Companies in SIC code 5164.

- 100 to 300 employees.

- Do all the buying at this location.

- Not affiliated with any national contracts.

With that profile, you can then go to a list broker and buy a list of companies in SIC 5164, with 100 to 300 employees, in your geographical area. Although that's not a perfect fit for your profile, it gets you close, and provides you with a list of suspects with whom to start.

Or you can solicit referrals from your customers. Once again, the language and phrasing of your questions can have a dramatic effect on your results. Instead of saying,

? Do you know anyone who could use my products? ?

ask,

? What other manufacturers do you know ?
who operate in the same segment you do,
and have 100 to 300 employees?

You'll find the specific question is easier for your customers to answer. Again, you may not get a perfect fit, but it will be a whole lot closer than just driving around and seeing who you can stumble across.

At some point you have a list of suspects. That is a starting point, but not an end. You'll need to continually add to that list as you collect information, talk with your customers, and are generally active within your territory.

2. You must qualify them, so you know they are the right people.

The next step is to collect some information about the account and hone in on the key individuals. If you have a lead, for example, let's assume that he has some interest in talking with you, or he wouldn't have been classified as a lead. So, he should be easier to get on the phone.

In the first phone conversation with a lead, the questions you ask can guide you to the information you'll need to make a decision about the investment of your sales time. Some better questions to help you determine whether or not they are worth your time are these:

? Can I ask what prompted your interest in this product/service? ?

? What role do you play in this? ?

? How important is this product/service to your company? ?

The answers to these questions should provide you with sufficient information to allow you to make a decision as to whether or not this individual is worth the investment of your sales time.

For those on your list of suspects who are not leads, you'll need to research them before you attempt to contact them. That means going to the Internet and gathering information, as well as talking to others who may know the account, and even calling the receptionist and asking for her help. A better question to use in that circumstance is this: "I'm sorry. Can you help me? I'm trying to find out...."

At some point, you will have learned enough about the suspect to determine that he is, at least tentatively, a qualified prospect. Now, your task is to make an appointment to see him.

3. You must engage with them.

At this point, you need to get an appointment for a dialogue with these people.

> ? I'd like to tell you about my products and my company. ?
>   Do you have 30 minutes tomorrow?

That, too often, is the kind of question salespeople ask in order to make a first appointment with a prospect. It's a horrible question. It is all about you. Why would anyone agree to spend 30 minutes of her precious time with someone she didn't know, and a company with which she was unfamiliar, listening to a description of a product for which she may not even have need?

Far better to ask something similar to this:

> We've worked with a number of companies like yours to
>   help them solve this problem [mention a problem you
> ? believe the prospect is likely to have]. I'll need about 15 ?
>   minutes of your time to see if there might be some
>   possibility that we could do the same for you. Would
>   tomorrow be okay, or would Wednesday be better?

One or two questions, asked by e-mail, fax, or phone, can grab the customer's interest and introduce you as a competent resource. Let's focus on that application. You want to make an appointment with someone who has never purchased from you, and who doesn't know you. Is that a place for "better questions?"

It is if you want to:

- Convey the perception of your competence.
- Show interest in the customer.
- Influence the customer to talk with you.

Let's examine some real questions proposed for this specific purpose by real salespeople. In my seminars, I'll often
break the class up into small groups and assign each group a
selling situation, and then ask them to create questions for that
situation. We then listen to the questions created by the small
groups, apply the criteria to them, and consider whether or not
they are better sales questions. The questions that follow in this
chapter, as well as several of the next chapters, were all developed in this way.

Let's start with the question I used to begin this chapter:

> I'd like to tell you about my products and my company.
> Do you have 30 minutes tomorrow?

This makes my top-10 list of the worst sales questions. The
question focuses solely on you and your agenda—what you
want. The customer really doesn't care what you want. The
question violates the first criterion in that it totally disregards
the customer's interests. It ignores the criterion that the question should reflect the depth of the relationship. In this case,
you have absolutely no relationship with the customer, yet you
are asking for 30 minutes of his time, which, in today's hectic
economic environment, is a major investment. Finally, it ends
with a yes or no, closed-ended question, which makes it easy for
the customer to say no to you. Far better to rephrase it this way:

> We've worked with a number of companies like yours to
> help them solve this problem.... I'd need about 15 minutes
> of your time to see whether or not there might be some
> possibility that we could do the same for you. Would
> tomorrow be okay, or would Wednesday be better?

This question begins with the customer, by referencing some problem you suspect she has. You would have had to do some research on her to know that, so it shows that you have already invested some time into the customer. It asks for a more reasonable amount of time, and it hints at a benefit to the customer. Finally, it offers the customer two different ways of saying yes. It's clearly a better question.

? What do you know about our company? ?

Not a bad question. It is open-ended, so it encourages the prospect to talk, and depending on the answer, may open the door for you to request an appointment. Even a short negative answer such as "Nothing" can be used as a segue into the next step: "It's for that reason I'd like to see you...."

? How much do you buy in this category? ?

This is a great example of a good question used at the wrong place in the sales process. Remember, we're trying to engage the customer sufficiently to convince him to see us, face-to-face. Although this question is perfectly appropriate in the early stages of the sales process, now is a bit too early. This is better saved for the next engagement.

? What do you expect from a supplier? ?

Another good example of the point I just made. Good question, but the wrong place in the sales process.

? How satisfied are you with your current vendor? ?

This is another for my list of all-time worst sales questions. First of all, who do you think picked the current vendor? Probably the person with whom you are talking, provided that you are talking to the right person. How likely is he to admit to making a mistake to someone he doesn't know, a company he hasn't dealt with, and a person he's never met? Ninety-nine out of 100 times, he is going to say he is satisfied. Having solicited this verbal affirmation from the customer, you are reduced to two strategies: One is to argue with him to show him that he is wrong, and that really your company is much better. That's a losing approach. The other is to pack up and go away, because, after all, you forced him to say that he was quite satisfied with his current vendor. Why, then, would he choose to spend any time with you?

So far, I've basically rejected a number of questions that have been proposed for this step in the sales process. Which leaves us wondering what *is* a good approach at this point.

Let's focus on the purpose: To build the customer's curiosity to the point at which he is willing to engage with you the first time in a face-to-face visit. This particular interchange is usually done over the phone, but may well be the result of a live cold call. That generally requires a bit of an introduction of your company. So anything you can ask that opens the door for this would be appropriate. The early question would work here:

? What do you know about [my company]? ?

If you have some common bond with the customer, that is always a good thing to bring up at this point. If you have done some work for a similar company, ask a question such as:

? Do you know [name of company]? ?

That's a closed-ended question, but it doesn't matter if the prospect answers yes or no. If, for example, she says no, then you go on to explain that the company is much like hers, tell her what you did for that company, and ask for an appointment. If she answers yes, then you can reply, "Good, then, as you know, that company is much like yours." Tell her. Mentioning some problem she is likely to have, and asking to what degree she may be dealing with that problem, is often an effective approach as well.

Regardless, your best strategy is to try to engage the customer with a question or two that gets her thinking about the possible benefits of talking with you. Once you have gained the appointment, you can move forward with the sales process.

Questions to Help You Make Them Comfortable With You

8 Helping your prospects and customers become comfortable with you is one of the practices of the best salespeople. Too many salespeople look at the selling opportunity as a technical problem to be solved, and focus all of their resources and attention on the "problem." They craft the most intricate solutions to their customers' problems, and wonder why the customer doesn't buy every time.

The *best* salespeople, however, understand the importance of the "people" element in sales, and know that the customer must be comfortable with the salesperson if the project is going to proceed in a positive way.

Without a level of comfort, the prospect will be guarded and tentative in his answers, and the salesperson cannot be assured that the information is full and accurate. The prospect will view the salesperson with some skepticism, and filter his conversation through that lens. On the other hand, if the prospect is comfortable with the salesperson, he will be much more likely to be forthcoming, honest, and accurate in the information provided to the salesperson.

Helping the prospect become comfortable with you, then, is a necessary step in the sales process. Some people call this "selling yourself before you sell the company."

In order to be comfortable with you, the prospect must know something of you and your company, must feel that you have some things in common, must perceive you as competent, and must believe that, to some degree, you are interested in him and willing to try to understand him. It is your job to implant these thoughts and feelings in the prospect's mind and heart. And, as always, a series of good questions is one of your best tools to do so.

One way people become comfortable with you is to feel that you are listening to them and care about them. To accomplish this, you'll need to ask some open-ended questions that prompt the customer to talk to you, and then to respond effectively to those comments. So, you would use a request such as:

? Tell me about your most pressing issues. ?

This is a nonthreatening, open-ended question that indicates you are interested in the customer's situation. It's easy for the customer to talk a bit in response to the question. And that provides you an opportunity to listen intently and then to demonstrate your interest by asking questions about the content in the customer's answer.

For example, let's say you are selling industrial chemicals to a manufacturer of health and beauty aids. You ask this question of your customer:

? Tell me about your most pressing issues. **?**

The customer talks about several items on her agenda, but mentions that recent federal regulations now require the company to lower the level of one component in one of its skin preparations. You reply to that content with a question similar to this:

? How urgent is it? **?**

The customer explains that the plant manager wants to have the change made within six months. Again, you demonstrate that you are listening and are concerned about the problem with a question such as this:

? What happens if you don't get this solved in the next few months? **?**

When the customer responds to this, you have gone a long way in accomplishing two things: You have made the customer comfortable with you by demonstrating your interest in her and listening intently to her responses. Secondly, you have uncovered an opportunity for you. It is not unusual for a good set of questions to contribute to more than one positive outcome. In this case, the positive outcome was a result of the combination of open-ended, customer-focused questions, followed by questions that demonstrated that you really do listen to the customer's concerns.

Another way to help people feel comfortable with you is to discover and then point out things you have in common. You do this by being sensitive to the customer and her environment, and asking about those items with which you may have some connection.

Perhaps my best example of this comes from a personal experience. I had an appointment with the owner of a small business to discuss training his salespeople. Upon meeting him, he asked if I would like a cup of coffee, and I, of course, said yes. He went out to retrieve the coffee, and that gave me a few moments to look around his office and find something we had in common.

When he came back with the coffee in hand, I pointed to a large photograph of a sailboat hanging on the wall. "Is that your boat?" I asked. "I sail too."

"Yes," he replied. I had just noticed something about him, asked about it, and then related that we had it in common. Classic.

The picture was very large, and I could read the name of the boat. It was too much of a coincidence to pass by, so I said, "Kelly Ann. My daughter's name is Kelly Ann." Another commonality.

He replied, "My daughter's name was Kelly Ann. She died early in life, and I named the boat after her."

"Oh," I said, "I'm sorry."

We then fell into a discussion of daughters, being a father, and sailing. Forty-five minutes later it was time to go and we hadn't yet gotten to business. Having achieved a significant personal bond, we made an appointment for a later date.

In this instance, it was my proactive practice that started the process of building what turned into a deep common bond. I took the time to notice something we had in common, ask about it, and then reflected on it. If I had not asked, I would not have made this customer comfortable with me and achieved the bond we clearly created with one another.

To help your customers feel comfortable with you, notice things about their environment, particularly if you sense that they had an effect on that environment, as in the photograph on the wall. One way to help you pick those things out is to ask yourself questions prior to the sales call. For example, you could say to yourself, "What in the office will I see that will provide me an opportunity to find something I have in common with him?" Just the process of asking yourself that question sharpens your senses, alerts your antenna to what you are looking for, and makes it much more likely that you will, in fact, find something that the two of you have in common.

When you are engaged with the prospect, the questions you ask him now become tantamount. Use questions similar to these:

? Is that yours? ?

? Do you...? ?

? There must be a story behind.... ?

? Tell me about.... ?

Notice also things about the person herself. Find an article of clothing to compliment, or something about her personal presentation to notice and ask about. For example, I recall meeting a gentleman who was wearing a large silver and turquoise ring. On his other hand, he had a similar silver and turquoise watch band. Clearly that was something he valued. My question?

? That's a beautiful watch band. Is there a story behind it? ?

When the customer explained that he had purchased it in an Indian reservation on a trip to the Southwest, I commented that I had been in that same place. And, like him, had also purchased some Indian jewelry. Common ground. Helping him be comfortable with me.

Another way to make people comfortable with you is to convey to the customer the perception of your competence. Customers want to know that the salespeople with whom they deal are competent. Again, it is your responsibility to convey that competence.

And the best way to do so is not by what you say, but rather by what you ask. Your ability to ask questions—detailed questions that probe the customer's specific issues and demonstrate a knowledge of his type of situations, his applications, and his type of companies, are those that best convey your competence.

Here's an example. Let's say you are selling hospital supplies to hospitals. One such product is suction tubing. You want to use your knowledge of suction tubing to ask questions that give the customer a perception of your competence—your knowledge of hospitals, suction tubing, and the uses and problems associated with it.

So, you put together a set of questions such as this:

> ? Many hospitals of your size use six to eight different configurations of suction tubing. Can I ask how many you use? ?

Notice that you have buffered the question with a statement of fact first to set up the situation, and then you asked the question. In addition to soliciting an important piece of information, you have conveyed the ideas that you know hospitals similar to this one, and you are familiar with suction tubing.

You follow that up with another similar question:

> ? Are you using sterile as well as non-sterile tubing in your E.R.? ?

To ask that question, you must know that E.R.'s often use both types. Therefore, you must have some experience with this situation.

Here's one more:

? A lot of people complain about how difficult it is to identify the length of the tubing from the packaging ? labels. They just look a lot alike. I wonder, to what degree is that an issue here?

That's a nice, soft question. It makes it easy to answer. And, again, it demonstrates your experience with the product.

Ask questions similar to these, and you accomplish several things: You collect pertinent information, and you convey your competence to the customer. Everyone wants to work with a competent salesperson, and no one wants to waste time with someone who is less than competent. By demonstrating your competence, you've gone a long way toward making people comfortable with you.

Questions to Help You Find Out What They Want— Generically

9

? How much are you currently paying? ?

Too often this question is the limit of the salesperson's information-collecting. It is one of the worst questions imaginable, in that it creates the perspective that the sale is only about price, and it prompts the customer to view the relationship through that perspective.

Finding out what the customer wants, in a broader and deeper sense, is the heart of the salesperson's job, and the most fundamental purpose of a series of good questions. It's here that the sales masters distinguish themselves from others.

Everything revolves around finding out what *they* want.

It is a clear and definable step in the sales process. You must have some idea what the customer wants so that you can craft your offer to meet that understanding. As such, this is the third, and the pivotal step in the sales process. Everything else revolves around it. It is the purpose for all of your work that went before. And it provides the framework for all of your work that follows.

However, finding out what they want is even larger than that. It is also something you do in every sales call throughout the process. You never stop finding out what they want, as you never have as full an understanding of it as you could.

So you would, in your first meeting with a prospect, try to find out as much of what he wanted as you could, given the constraints of time. And, in your second meeting, you'd focus entirely on finding out what he wanted. When you present your offer, you'd constantly test his reactions as a way of further refining your understanding of what he wanted. And so on. Some part of every interaction will involve you finding out what they want in a broader and deeper sense.

If you can't do this, you shouldn't be in sales. You need a minimum competency at this, or you should be doing something else. But just because you have a minimum competency, it doesn't mean you are as good at this core skill as you could be. Like everything else, you can become better at finding out what they want. And the primary way you do that is to ask better questions.

For our purposes, we're going to deal with this in three ways:

1. Finding out what a prospect wants in order to make an offer for his first purchase.

2. When a customer provides you an opportunity, you need to find out what he wants in a deeper and broader sense so that you can fill those needs.

3. In working with a regular customer, finding out
    what he wants in order to uncover additional
    opportunities for your goods and services.

In Chapter 10, we look at questions for situation number
one, a cold call. In Chapter 11, we examine questions to understand an opportunity, and in Chapter 12 we deal with questions
to uncover additional opportunities with a regular customer.

This is such an important part of the salesperson's challenge that there are some additional criteria for better questions
that are specific to just this situation. If you are going to ask
better questions at this stage, in addition to the basic criteria for
a better question, you'll also need to think of "broader and
deeper."

Your "finding out what they want" questions should seek
information that is *broader* than what other people think, and
collects information that is *deeper* than the normal. If you are
able to understand your customer in a broader and deeper way,
you'll have an immense advantage over your competition. That
is what makes a better question at this point in the process.

Broader means that you gain a big-picture understanding
of this customer and how this particular need fits into the larger
scheme. I like the acronym one of my clients developed to capture this part of the process: You must know the customer's
SONG. SONG stands for Situation, Organization, Norms, and
Goals.

Understanding the customer's *situation* means that your
questions seek to uncover where the customer is today, relative
to her goals, finances, customers, and competition. For example,
it's one thing if the customer is way ahead of her plan for the
year, and it is an entirely different situation if she is way behind. It's one thing if the customer is flush with cash, quite
another if she's behind on all her bills. These things will have a
great effect on the solution you eventually offer this customer.

Organization refers to the understanding of who the key
people are in this account, relative to the issue in which you

are interested. Who are the decision-makers, and who are their bosses? Who actually uses the product or service? Who has an interest in it? Who signs the check, issues the P.O., receives the goods?

Norms refers to the customers' values and procedures. Is this primarily a "low price" account, or do they value service in their dealings with their suppliers? What is their image of themselves? Are they market leaders or bottom feeders? And what are their procedures? How is a decision made? How is it implemented?

Goals are self-explanatory: What do they want to accomplish in the short term with this particular purchase, and in the long run for their business or organization?

When you understand those things you understand the customer *broadly*. Clearly, your questions need to reflect this perspective.

But you aren't done yet. Sales masters focus on understanding their customer deeply as well. A good way to understand the concept of "deep" is to review the "peeling the onion" analogy from Chapter 1. Our knowledge of the customer is like peeling an onion—there are layers of depth of understanding, just as there are layers to the onion. On the surface, your understanding of the customer is superficial, much like the skin of the onion. It doesn't have much power or substance to it. That's where most salespeople operate. They focus on the "technical specifications" of the customer's needs. How many, what kind, delivered when, at what price? Just as it is necessary to peel the skin of the onion before you can penetrate deeper, so too it is necessary to collect the superficial information before you can penetrate deeper.

The real trick is to methodically peel the onion layer after layer, and understand the deeper underlying factors—the attitudes, values, emotions, and goals that shape the specific need about which the customer is talking to you. Here's a way to visualize this—it's my onion simplified. Think of peeling the onion in a few simple levels by understanding the customer's PIE.

"P" stands for *problems/objectives*. In other words, what is the customer trying to achieve with this specific purchase? Is it to solve some problem? To make some pain go away? Or is it to achieve some objective? To move the organization to a more positive place? When you understand that, you have peeled the onion to a greater degree than 90 percent of your competitors, because you have moved beyond the superficial technical specifications, and begun to dig into the reasons why.

"I" stands for *implications*. When you uncover the implications for the customer, you have a graphic and detailed knowledge of what this deal, this problem, or this application means to the customer. You'll know what benefit it brings to the company, and what benefit a successful resolution brings to the individuals involved in the decision. You'll also be aware of the opposite effect. What consequences will afflict the company if this transaction is not successful? What price will the individuals pay if this isn't resolved positively?

Finally, "E" stands for *emotions*. How does all this make the key people feel? If this person—a decision-maker—causes a positive effect on the company, what will he feel? And if the decision isn't a good one, and brings negative consequences, how will that make him feel?

If you can dig deeper in your conversations with the customer, and peel the onion to the extent that you understand the PIE for the customers, you'll have a clear advantage over your competitors, who are probably busy figuring out how they can drop their price.

Let me give you an example of digging deeper to discover the customer's PIE. Let's say that you are selling telephone systems, and your customer owns a small business that needs an updated system for 12 people.

Your customer says, "Can you quote me on a system for 12 people?"

You say, "Sure." (This is where most salespeople stop. Superficial information and superficial response. They rush out to prepare a quote that meets the customer's technical specifications.) You, however, peel the onion and dig deeper. So you ask,

? Do you mind if I ask a few questions first? ?

"No," the customer responds. "Go ahead."

? How urgent is this? Is your current system malfunctioning? ?

(This is both a technical-spec type of question, trying to understand the time frame of the customer's need, and a lead into a deeper question.) The customer replies, "No, we're not having any equipment problems at the moment. So I'm not in any hurry. Some time in the next couple of weeks would be fine."

You say,

? If you aren't having any equipment problems, what prompts your interest in new system at this point? ?

(This is you digging at the P—problems and objectives—level.) The customer replies, "Our current system is obsolete. For example, callers can't leave a voice message for individuals. There are other issues besides that, but that gives you an idea."

? So, it's really not a matter of new hardware. What you really want to do is gain some additional capabilities with this purchase. Would that be right? ?

The customer replies, "Yes, I suppose you are right."
You reply,

? Have you thought about what capabilities you'd want, in addition to the voice-mail issue you mentioned? ?

The customer says, "Not really. What's available?"
You reply,

> I'll go through a menu with you. Just a couple more questions. How important is this to you? If you don't get these new capabilities, how will that affect the company?

Your customer replies, "I'm sure that we are losing customers because of the lack of convenience in the voice-mail issue. So, it's costing us real money to continue with our current system. And my employees are continually frustrated with the clunkiness of the current system."

You reply,

> So there is a lot of frustration?

Your customer says, "Yep."

Now, let's stop here and see what we've done. The typical salesperson will reply to the customer's first question, "Can you quote a system?" and send him a quote, call two weeks later to follow up, and complain about having to be the low price.

Our master salesperson approached the situation with an eye on uncovering the customer's PIE before he proposed anything. He learned this:

> **Problem:** The current system doesn't have the features he wants. It's not about the hardware, it's about the features.

> **Implications:** The current system is causing the company to lose customers. That's a real, economically measurable cost.

> **Emotions:** Everyone is frustrated.

The master salesperson can now say something similar to this:

?   I can offer you a solution that will end all that frustration
and actually be a joy to use. And, because your real issue
is the features and capabilities, we can program that
into a master unit, and not need to replace every
handset. It'll take me about 45 minutes to describe
the solution for you. Do you have time Tuesday of
next week, or is Wednesday better?   ?

The customer replies, "Sounds interesting. Let's do it Tuesday."

Which of these two salespeople do you think has the better chance of getting this business? The one who replied with a quote, or the one who took the time to uncover the customer's PIE?

Do you see how important this is? It truly is the pivotal skill for a master salesperson. Let the rest of the world content themselves with superficial answers to superficial questions. You uncover the customer's SONG and PIE.

Questions to Help You Find Out What They Want— In a First Visit

10

The first visit to a new prospect (or, in other words, a cold call) is one of those times that requires your best efforts. If you are successful, you will have sufficiently intrigued the customer to inspire her to see you again. If not, the relationship is likely to go no further.

From the sales process perspective, there are always two fundamental objectives in a first call on a new prospect. One of them is to collect additional information— sufficient information to test your judgment that the account is qualified and worth your investment of time. You may even want to collect sufficient information to rate the prospect on our rating system. (See *10 Secrets of Time Management for Salespeople*, Chapter 4.)

The second objective is to get a second appointment. That's it. Without a second appointment, your entire sales process is derailed. In a second appointment, your status is completely different: You have some history with the prospect; he has indicated an interest in what you have; you have learned something more about him; you are operating with the benefit of a deeper relationship. A second appointment is the absolute number-one objective for a first appointment.

You gain a second appointment by suggesting something the prospect is going to get in the second appointment that may be of benefit to her. At this point, she is not going to see you again because of your dramatic good looks, awesome sense of humor, or penetrating insights. That can come later. For now, she has to expect to get something for her investment of time. Your job is to uncover enough of what is happening with this prospect in the first meeting that you can intelligently and honestly suggest (or imply) something she is going to receive in the second meeting.

That means you must ask questions to uncover it. But not just any questions—your chances of gaining a second appointment are dramatically increased by asking *better* questions. So your questions should be designed to accomplish any or all of these:

- Collect sufficient information in order to qualify (or rate) the prospect.
- Identify his situation.
- Identify some of his needs/interests.
- Identify some point of pain.
- Expose some motivation.
- Seek an opportunity for a personal connection.
- Show your competence.

You don't need to do all of these. Often, if you hit on one that has some passion behind it, you'll have done well. Unfortunately, you don't know which one excites the customer, so you'll need to prepare for all of them.

Before I suggest some questions for this stage of the sales process, let's look at some questions suggested by real salespeople in my seminars.

? What part of your product line do you produce here? ?

I'm a little ambiguous about this question. On one hand, it is inquisitive of the customer, easy for her to answer, and opens up the topic of conversation. On the other hand, more and more customers are expecting you to know what they do before you call on them. This question shows that you did not do much homework on the customer, and can put her off a little as a result.

? From whom are you buying now? ?

? What do you like about your current supplier? ?

? What do you not like about your current supplier? ?

I put these three together because of their similarity. The salespeople who suggested these questions must have gone to the same sales school as most of the salespeople in my seminars, as these questions are regularly put forward.

Each of these questions focuses on the competition, not the customer. They force the customer to think about the competition, violating one of our criteria for a better sales question. Do you really want him to think about the competitor? Let him do that on his time, not on yours.

At the same time, these questions reveal negative things about you. The number-one reason you want to know from whom the customer is buying is that it gives you an idea of where you have to be price-wise. Your customers are sophisticated enough to know that. In so doing, you have unintentionally and indirectly put price into the equation right away. These questions reveal your mindset as that of a peddler, not a professional, consultative salesperson.

Far better to ask something similar to this:

? What do you look for in a supplier? ?

That is a question about the customer, not the competition. It shows interest in the customer's values, and respect for the customer's priorities. It's a better question.

? What are you paying now? ?

EEK! This is a horrible question. Review my previous comments. You have shown the customer that your whole approach is going to be about price. If you start the conversation off this way, don't complain to me that your customers keep pressuring you for a lower price.

? Can you tell me about the application? ?

I like this question. It is an open-ended question, which is often effective at this stage of the sales process. It will get the customer talking. And the tone is a little deferential. All good stuff.

? What is your role in the organization? ?

This question may be good as the very first qualifier, if you are not sure if the person you are meeting with is a qualified decision-maker. In that role, it is much better than the oft-proposed "Who makes the decision here?" This allows the customer to answer in the positive, and provides you the information you need.

> **? Do you know how many branches we have in our company? ?**

Who cares? Clearly the person who is asking this question wants to open up the opportunity to tell the customer how many branches the company has. Yawn.

If the customer says, "Yes, I do." That stops the conversation right there. If the customer says no, then the salesperson can jump in and say, "We have [x number of] branches." So what? This is the kind of question that makes the salesperson appear stuck on herself, and takes up the customer's time for no good reason. If you want him to know how many branches you have, just tell him. Don't go through this ritual.

> **? How long have you worked for the company? ?**

I think this question is bit too much for the first call. Remember, the purpose of a first call is to gain a second visit. It's too personal and extraneous for the first visit. If you are using this question to show some interest in the individual and get him talking, it doesn't work very well.

Because it is a closed-ended question, it can easily be answered in a couple words: "Five years." That doesn't prompt her to talk much. If that were the purpose of the question, it would be better to open it up, and ask something similar to this:

> **? Tell me a little about your history with the company. ?**

**? Have you investigated the possibility ?
of buying from overseas?**

In this case, the salesperson is representing an importer, and wants to probe for the customer's position relative to the source of his products. It really is an extraneous question, introducing what could be a negative into the conversation. Who cares if the company has or has not investigated the possibility?

If the customer says yes, it opens you up to the possibility of a follow-up thought: "and we've ruled it out." This now effectively shuts you down before you even have an opportunity to describe your product. Because of that possibility, I wouldn't use this question. Why point out the issues related to your product this early in the relationship? Better to find a problem the customer has and focus on that, than to begin the conversation with your product issues.

? How do you go about making a decision? ?

If you subscribe to my view that the purpose of a first call is to get a second call, then this question is a bit out of place on the first call. It really is extraneous information that you don't need at this point. Asking it takes you off focus. Better to give them a reason to see you again, and use this on the second call.

**? How would you describe your ?
current purchasing structure?**

Not a bad question. It helps you determine with whom you should be meeting, and probes for that information in a soft, open-ended format.

**? What are the top three competencies ?
you value in a supplier?**

Another good question. It calls on the customer to share her values with you, and provides you some substance upon which to build.

> **? What contracts are currently in ?
> existence with your suppliers?**

This is a qualifying question. If the prospect answers in a way that indicates that all of the areas you address are under three-year contracts with competitors, you may be better off investing your time elsewhere. Better to make that decision as early in the sales process as possible to save your time.

> **? What would be the best way for me to ?
> present our products and services?**

Not a bad question. On the plus side, it shows respect for the prospect and draws him into the project. On the negative side, it implies that you will follow his direction. For example, in one of my sales positions, I sold surgical staplers to surgeons in the operating room. It was absolutely mandatory that we get to the operating room supervisor and gain her permission to work with the surgeons in the OR.

I wouldn't have asked this question, because of the chance the purchasing person to whom I was addressing the question would say something such as: "We never allow salespeople to call on the department heads. Everything goes through me." Now, I've put myself in the position of directly contradicting his direction if I'm going to sell in this hospital. I've put myself in an untenable position by asking the wrong question.

Here's my list of a few better sales questions for a first call on a prospect.

? How much are you going to spend on ?
[my category of product] this year?

This is one of those qualifying questions that provides you with extremely important information. Remember, one of the purposes of a first call is to collect information upon which you can make a determination as to whether or not this customer is worth your time. You need to ask this question in order to collect that information.

? Tell me a little about what you look for in a vendor. ?

This is a nice, soft, open-ended question that really probes into the prospect's philosophy. This is really a qualifying question, in that it provides you information on which to make the decision as to whether or not this prospect is worth your time.

For example, if he says, "All we care about is low prices and delivery on time," then you can safely assume that the prospect is more interested in price than partnership. If your value in the market has little to do with being the low price, it may be that this prospect is not for you!

? In regard to the kinds of products/services I sell, ?
what are some of your most pressing challenges?

This is an open-ended question that shows respect for the customer, and offers him an opportunity to describe a need or problem to you. It probes for some point of pain. If the customer responds by describing at least one issue you can solve, follow up with this question:

? What are some of the implications to the company? ?
How important is that?

At this point, you have all you need to prompt a second visit. Tell her you have some solutions for that issue, and you'd like to take a little more time to describe them to her. Ask for a second visit.

If you can't uncover some pain, then you need to fall back to uncovering a less passionate need. One way to do this is to discuss, in general terms, the breadth of products/services your company offers, and then ask something similar to this:

? Which of these areas holds the most interest to you? ?

This is an assumptive question that asks the prospect to state his priority. I always prefer that line of questioning because it can reveal the customer's goals, values, and critical points of concern. Notice that you didn't ask, "Do any of these hold an interest for you?" which allows the prospect the latitude to say no. This question calls for a choice, but not a yes or no.

? If you had some issues with your current situation, which of these would be most likely to pop up on your radar screen? ?

This is very similar to the question preceding it. It calls on the prospect to uncover his highest-priority interest. Nice question. Notice that it asks for "which" one, not a yes or no.

If either of these questions has surfaced an issue, then you can follow up with this question:

? What are the implications of that? ?

Or, more to the point,

? How important would that be to your company? ?

Once again, if you have gained something solid in your prospect's conversation, it's time to ask for a second appointment to discuss your response to her stated issues.

? Why are you taking time to see me now? ?

This is one of my all-time best sales questions. It penetrates to the heart of the onion right away, cutting down to the issue of motivation and allowing the customer the opportunity to describe his situation. It is an open-ended question that prompts the customer to explain. It puts the key issue right on the table, and may be the only question you need to ask to uncover a significant opportunity.

? What's your current situation with regard to this issue? ?

This is a bit risky for a first call, because it assumes a degree of familiarity that may not be there. At first, it looks like a question I never ask, "What do you not like about your current vendor?" Notice, though, that it asks about the customer's situation, *not* the current vendor. The customer can choose to tell you about issues related to the current vendor, but your question did not force her to that line of thinking. Because it is a bit more open-ended, it allows for the conversation to go in a number of ways. If things are going well, and you seem to be clicking with the prospect, this will probe for some area of motivation.

? To what degree do you have to deal with [an issue that is common for this kind of organization]? ?

This is a competence-conveying question. It illustrates your knowledge of the market and the prospect's situation. It shows interest in the prospect as well. Good question. If he offers some meat in his response, you have something with which to work.

? What are some of the challenges that are high on your list today? ?

This is an easy question for the customer to answer, shows that you are interested in her, and, hopefully, begins to uncover a need with which you may be able to help. All of that makes it a good sales question for this situation.

Notice also the choice of the word *challenges*. A lot of salespeople ask about *problems*. I think *challenges* is better. *Problems* has a negative connotation to it. To admit to having problems can make the customer feel badly about himself, and he may not want to answer that question truthfully. Substituting the word *challenges* broadens the scope of the question, and removes the negative connotation.

In a first call on a prospect, the language in your questions is probably more important than in any other call. Ask better questions, and your prospects of gaining a second visit, and eventually a new customer, are greatly increased. Ask poor questions, and the likelihood of you being invited back is minimal.

Questions to Help You Find Out What They Want—In a Specific Opportunity

11

This is probably the most common situation for salespeople, and one in which the effective use of better sales questions can make all the difference in your ability to provide the customer with a solution that will bring you the business.

The situation is this: You are interacting with a customer and you have identified a specific opportunity. It could take many forms. It may be something as pedestrian as the customer asking you for a price or showing interest in a product you handle, to something as challenging as the customer inviting you to discuss a new project in its infancy.

Regardless, it is in this scenario that the best salespeople can distinguish themselves from their competitors by digging as deeply into the opportunity as possible. It really is the place where peeling the onion provides you an advantage.

The world is full of superficial and mediocre salespeople who respond to the customer's request in a superficial manner. For example, the customer may say that she is considering a new project, and asks for your price. The superficial salesperson rushes to quote the price, and wonders why the customer doesn't buy.

The professional salesperson understands that the customer's request for a price is the superficial expression of a deeper issue, and takes time to dig deeper (with better questions) to uncover the issue as a deeper level.

Here's an example.

One of my clients had asked me to work with his salespeople to help them "close the sale." I decided to ride with a couple of salespeople to assess their competency. I soon discovered that the issue wasn't closing the sale, it was opening it!

The company was a commercial HVAC contractor. I accompanied one salesperson on a sales call for which he had an appointment. The prospect, who had called the company, was waiting for us.

"We added additional office space a few years ago," he explained, "but we never added additional air-conditioning capacity. So it has always been warm and stuffy in the new section of the office. I guess we want to do something about it now."

The salesperson asked to see the new wing of the office building. There, he took out a note pad and measuring tape, and dutifully measured every room in the new space, taking detailed notes. Next, he asked the prospect if he could see the existing air conditioner.

"It's up in the attic," the prospect said. "It's kind of dusty up there, but I can show it to you."

The three of us climbed the stairs to the attic. There was a platform at the top of the steps, which supported several boxes of old files and ancient records. The better part of the attic, however, was composed of exposed beams with insulation stuffed between them. Off in a corner was another platform on which the air conditioner rested.

I chit-chatted with the customer as the salesperson carefully maneuvered over the beams to the platform and inspected the air-conditioning equipment. After making more notes, he came back to where I was standing with the prospect.

"Okay," he said, "I have what I need. How about if I fax you a proposal within 24 hours?"

"That would be okay," the prospect said.

It was clear to me at this point that the salesperson had done an excellent job of capturing the technical specifications, and had done absolutely nothing to dig any deeper into the opportunity.

I said to the prospect, "I have a couple of questions." He said, "Okay."

"If you like our quote, what is the likelihood that you'll buy it within the next couple of weeks?"

"None at all," he said. "I'm just collecting information for the boss. He wants to put it on the budget for next year."

"So, you don't need a detailed quote faxed to you?"

"No, just a ballpark price will do for now."

I looked at the salesperson and said, "What's a ballpark price?"

"About $4,000" he said.

"Thanks" said the prospect.

"Help me understand something," I asked. "When we came in, you indicated that the offices had been built some time ago, but that it was only now that you wanted to do something about the air conditioning. What's changed to make this an issue now?"

"Yeah, it has always been stuffy in the new office. Remember a couple weeks ago when we had that heat spell?"

"Yes," we all agreed.

"Well, the air conditioning worked so hard that it actually froze up. We had to unplug the unit to allow the ice to melt off it. The ice melted, formed a pool on the platform, and evidently spilled over the side, through the insulation, through the ceiling below, onto the president's desk!"

"So, what you really want is to make sure that doesn't happen again!"

"Yep," he said.

"One last question," I said. "What can we do to make you look good in all of this?"

"I'm not going to make the decision. In this business, the boss makes all of these kinds of decisions. I'm just collecting information for him."

"So the boss makes the decision. Do you suppose we could see him?"

"Sure," he said, "let me see if he's available."

In this case, the salesperson had done a great job of collecting the technical specifications, but had absolutely no idea what the customer was really looking for, who would make the decision, or how or when a decision would be made. He'd work hard at creating the quote, fax it to the prospect, and then wonder why the company didn't buy.

To gain a better understanding of the opportunity, the salesperson should have peeled the onion and asked more questions. Let's look at questions for this situation proposed to me by real salespeople in my seminars.

? Is there anything else I should know? ?

This is on my list of the best sales questions. It implies a certain level of competence on your part, in that you assume that the customer wants you to know certain things about him. That means that the customer sees you as a potential supplier— otherwise why would he want you to know anything? It is a closed-ended question, but it is perfectly appropriate. If he says yes, he will explain what else he wants you to know. If he says no, then you are free to segue onto the next issue. I use this question frequently when I'm trying to "find out what they want." It's how I put an end to that conversation.

? **What other products are you buying, and from whom?** ?

I can see a place for the first part of this question. When you apply our onion analogy to it, you'll recognize that the question is "skin of the onion"; a superficial question about technical specifications. However, there is a time and place for collecting that information, and this is an appropriate way to ask about it. What I don't like is the "from whom" portion. Again, you prompt the customer to think about the competition, and I'd rather she do that on her own time, not on mine. It raises the possibility of forcing the customer into a defensive position. If you are interested in the customer, what possible difference does it make from whom she is buying? The main reason you want to know that is to gain a sense of what the customer is paying for the product so that you can quote a lower price. That's you interjecting price into the conversation without knowing you are doing it.

? **How many dollars are you going to allocate for the project?** ?

Of course you must ask this question in one way or another. It's the qualifying question. If the customer answers it, you'll have an idea of what he has allocated for the solution, which is an important piece of information. You'll be able to adjust your solution based on this. If he doesn't answer, you haven't hurt yourself by asking it.

? Anything not on the specs that the director
would like to have in the project? ?

This is clearly a question for a specific situation—in this
case, a seller of materials for construction projects. I like the question because it does a couple of things. First, it is a competency-
creating question, as it demonstrates to the customer that you
know that often there are things the customer would like to
have, but didn't get on the specifications. How would you know
that? Only by experience. So this question demonstrates your
experience. Secondly, if the customer answers in the affirmative, you'll be able to gain an edge on your competition by
quoting items that fall into this category, whereas the competition may only quote the specs.

? What are your priorities with regard to this issue? ?

This is a good question. Stop a minute and revisit the onion
in Chapter 2. Into what level of the onion does this question
dig? Clearly it is about the customer's deeper priorities and
goals. It shows real concern for the customer, and uncovers
some significant motivation. If you get an honest answer, you
may have all you need to separate your solution from the
competition's.

? What can we do to help you succeed? ?

I'm a little ambivalent about this question. The problem is
that the customer may answer with something that you cannot
possibly do. In that case, you have interjected a needless negative into the situation. On the other hand, it does probe for the
customer's personal motivation. I'd prefer a better question,
such as this:

? What's going to be necessary for you
to be successful in this instance? ?

This should uncover the same information without opening the possibility of committing yourself to something you can't do. It's a better question.

? What are some of the biggest mistakes ?
past suppliers have made?

I'm a bit ambivalent about this question. I generally don't like directing the customer to think about the competion, whether it is negative or positive. In this case, it's not exactly about the competion; it's about the competition's mistakes. The customer could answer without identifying od of your competitors. But, it does turn the conversation in a negative direction and, perhaps, put the customer off. What information could you gain by it that you don't already have? I'd pass on this one.

? What is the most important factor when ?
purchasing [x product] from a vendor?

Generally, I like questions that ask for the customer to prioritize, as this one does, by asking for the "most important factor." You'll get the customer to think about priorities, and perhaps to verbally commit to something other than price. If so, you'll be able to build your solution and your presentation on information that the customer provides in the answer to this question.

? Tell me a bit about how your ?
decision-making process works.

Good question. It gets the customer thinking about a process. That's good. It is soft and unthreatening, and provides information you need to know if you are going to move forward.

This is a place where your understanding of the onion will most come into play. In a smaller opportunity, focus on understanding the customer's PIE as it relates to this specific need.

In a larger opportunity, peel the onion as deeply as you can, listening for information that can provide you a competitive edge— pieces of information on which you can build your situation.

Questions to Help You Follow Up

12

The idea of questions to *follow up* assumes that something has occurred prior to you asking these kinds of questions, and that the questions you ask reference that event. Every time you present something to a customer, that presentation has an effect on the customer—he thinks or feels something about what you said. Master salespeople understand the power of clearly understanding those thoughts and feelings. The more you understand the customer, the more able you are to provide attractive solutions to him.

There are two specific applications for these kinds of questions. The first is to assess the customer's response to a proposal or presentation you have made. The second application is a bit broader—to follow up after the purchase, on the customer's degree of satisfaction. (We are going to deal with this application in Chapter 14.)

Think about all the times you present some information to the customer. Here's a list of some of them:

- In a cold call, when you present your company.

- Whenever you answer a customer's question.

- When you present an idea or suggestion that may lead to a more in-depth presentation later.

- When you suggest an appointment to deal with some issue.

- When your customer has a problem, and you offer a solution.

- When you present your product or proposal.

- When you respond to the customer's concerns about your proposal.

In each of these situations, you have provided some information, and that information has affected the customer in some way. Your job now is to assess the customer's reactions.

In one sense, these questions often overlap with those in Chapters 9, 10, and 11, because your purpose is similar—"to find out what they want." But, because of this unique situation, these questions can take a different form. You are finding out what they want relative to what you have just presented to them. Another way to think of it is this: You are finding out if this (your presentation) is what they want.

Once again, in addition to the basic criteria for all good sales questions, there are some unique issues and criteria for this particular situation:

1. To make sure you do ask, so that you gain an understanding of your customers' thoughts and feelings.

2. To ask at deeper levels. If you do not uncover deeper concerns, many of your proposals will never be acted upon.

The first issue reflects the most common fault of salespeople when it comes to this situation. They neglect to ask—they don't probe into the customer's reactions—so they go away from the sales call without a definitive understanding of where the customer is.

It may be that they are afraid of the possible rejection—that the proposal really doesn't excite the customer. Or it may be that they have never been trained in asking these kinds of questions. Regardless, before you can ask *better* questions, you must first ask *a* question.

The sales masters do more than just ask a question. They ask better questions by attempting to uncover the deeper issues. *Deeper issues* refers to the reason underneath the reason—the attitudes and thoughts that support and give rise to initial verbalized responses. It is not unusual for a customer to reply with a superficial response. Sometimes, it is because he doesn't want to make a commitment, and sometimes because he doesn't want to interject a negative into the conversation. Still others may not want to have a discussion with you about it, because they have already made up their minds to do something else.

Let's look at some questions from real salespeople for such a situation.

? Do you have any questions about our product? ?

This is the instinctive follow-up question. It's okay. I suppose you have to ask it. I much prefer a broader, open-ended question such as this:

? What concerns might you have about implementing this? ?

Concerns is broader than *questions,* allowing more room for the customer's input. His concerns may not be related to product—he may have concerns about his people's ability to learn to use it. Your previous question may not have surfaced that issue, whereas this one would. The use of the word *implementing* is assumptive in that it goes past the decision as to whether or not to buy it, and puts the real issue on the table. This is a better question.

? Does this meet your expectations? ?

This is a commonly used closed-ended question. I don't like it, because it gives the customer latitude to answer with a definitive no. If that's the case, then you have to regroup and work from a negative position to make any headway. I prefer you change that question to this one:

? To what degree does this meet your expectations? ?

Once again, your customer may say, "Not at all." But you haven't forced her to voice that position by the language in your question. This question gives the customer more room to nuance her response, which in turn gives you more information upon which to build your reply.

? Will this benefit you? ?

This is exactly the same kind of question as the previous one. For this same reason, it is better asked this way:

? To what degree do you see this benefiting you? ?

? What do you think? ?

A good question. It's open-ended and nonthreatening, and sincerely wants to understand the customer's reaction. It is best used with someone who is task-oriented, as opposed to someone who is people-oriented. For that person, I prefer the question,

? How do you feel about this? ?

? What areas do you need us to clarify further? ?

Not a bad question. I think it's better than "Do you have any questions?"

Let's examine some scenarios and identify better questions.

1. In a cold call, when you present your company.

Prior to presenting your company's story, I like to find out what the prospect knows through this question:

? What do you know about our company? ?

This will give you some idea of the prospect's experience, or lack thereof, with your company. It provides a nice starting point for your description of your company.

After you have presented your company's story, a question similar to this is a good way to segue way back into probing the prospect's issues:

? To what degree do you see yourself ?
    using companies like mine?

The "companies like mine" generalizes the response, and doesn't force the customer to comment on your own organization. It provides you with the information you want, and should provide you something upon which to build.

2. Whenever you answer a customer's question.

Here's a question to ask after you have answered a question:

? Okay? ?

This simple interrogative inquires into two things: Whether or not the customer understood the answer, and whether or not the answer was what the customer wanted to hear. In either case, it's information you need.

3. When your customer has a problem with your company or your product, and you offer a solution.

? How does that sound? ?

This puts the issue squarely on the table, and solicits, in an open-ended fashion, the customer's reaction. Good question.

4. After you have presented your solution, product, or proposal.

Try this sequence:

? How does that sound? ?

This is a wide open question that just probes for whatever feedback your customers want to provide, and typically will uncover that issue at the top of their minds. It's nonthreatening, and doesn't force customers into a corner. If they respond with

any kind of depth, this is a great place to then ask the ubiqui-
tous follow-up question:

? Anything else? ?

? To what degree does this match ?
       what you were looking for?

This is a more specific question that narrows in on the ultimate issue. Yet it's asked in a way that makes it nonthreatening
and inquisitive. I prefer it to be used after the first one.

? How do you see yourself implementing this? ?

If you are receiving favorable responses for the first two
questions, then this one bridges the gap from thoughts to actions. Get a positive response from them once, and it's time to
close.

Questions to Help You Gain Agreement

13

"Closing the sale" is the most overrated and over-hyped portion of the sales process. The world of sales training literature is filled with dozens of treatments of "how to close the sale." Too many people separate it from the rest of the sales process, and treat it as an added-on appendage at the end of the sales cycle.

That's too bad. If you methodically gain agreement at every step of the process, the actual decision to buy is a natural and logical outcome of everything that went before. Gaining agreement is not just for the final purchase order; it's a mindset and a process in which you engage at every sales call, at every stage of the sales process.

It is not a matter of cleverly manipulating the customer so that he says yes to you when you want him to say it. It is not a struggle with the customer to gain the upper hand and "overcome" the customer's reluctance. It is simply a matter of seeing the situation from the customer's point of view, of understanding the next step in the customer's buying process, and then putting the issue of committing to take the next step on the table.

For example, if you call a prospect for an appointment, the next step is to grant you the appointment. Once in a face-to-face meeting with the prospect, the next step is to gain a second meeting. In that meeting, the next step would be to grant you an opportunity to present your solution. At that meeting, the next step may be to purchase a sample. After that, the next step may be to try a beginning inventory of your product. At each meeting, the focus of the meeting and your "closing" is to gain an agreement for the next step of the process.

Gaining agreement with the customer for the next step, whatever that may be, is a skill that marks the best salespeople. As in every part of the sales process, there are questions that facilitate the process, and some are better than others.

In addition to the criteria for any sales question (which we developed in Chapter 3), there are two additional primary issues here:

1. To actually ask the question, rather than let the sales call end without any resolution.
2. To ask the question in a way that is non-manipulative, and doesn't put the customer on the defensive.

Let's discuss the first: actually asking the question. Probably the number-one fault of salespeople, when it comes to the face-to-face portion of their job, is to leave a sales call without any resolution. It's just so easy to avoid that moment of possible rejection. So we shake hands and go on, assuming the call was successful, and hoping the customer will do something to move the project forward. After all, we thought we made a good presentation or had a good conversation.

Here's an example: You are in the middle of a cold call with a qualified prospect, and have presented your capability brochure as a way to tell her about your company. The prospect says, "This looks interesting, but I don't have any more time right now. Can you send me some additional information?" You say sure and shake hands to leave. You walk out thinking you did a good thing.

However, you didn't bring the sales call to any conclusion. There was no "close." My definition of a close is this: *An agreement for action that always involves the customer agreeing to do something that moves the project forward.*

In this situation, what did the prospect agree to do? Nothing. You agreed to send her some literature, but she didn't agree to do anything.

Let's revisit this situation, this time bringing it to resolution. The situation is the same, and the prospect says the same thing: "This looks interesting, but I don't have any more time right now. Can you send me some additional information?" You say,

> ? Sure. I'll put it in the mail tomorrow. You should have it by Monday. How about if we schedule 15 minutes on the phone to discuss it? Will Tuesday afternoon work for you, or is Wednesday better? ?

You have now asked for some agreement with the prospect on some action she will take. If she says okay to your request for an appointment, you have closed that part of the sales process, and moved the project forward. If she says no, you know where you stand right now, and won't be tempted to waste hours and hours in voice mail trying to get an appointment with someone who isn't interested.

Because of this all-too-common syndrome, I have formulated my first rule for closing: Always ask for action.

That means just what it says. In every interaction with a prospect or customer, ask for some agreement on the action he or will take as a result of the sales call. If there is no appropriate action, then you should not have made the sales call. An agreement for action is the very definition of a sales call: an interaction between the salesperson and the customer designed to create an action on the part of the customer.

Every phone call, every live visit, every time you talk to a customer, make it a practice of asking for action. A *better* question is one that is asked, as opposed to those that never issue forth from the lips.

The second challenge for us in closing the sale is to ask the question in a way that is non-manipulative, and doesn't put the customer on the defensive. For example, a question such as this is often proposed as a "good" closing question:

> If I could save you 4 percent, is there any reason why you would not buy this now?

My view is that it is horribly manipulative, creates a defensive response on the part of the customer, and reveals the salesperson to be much more concerned with his numbers than solving the customer's problems. I'd much prefer something similar to this:

> To what degree does this look like it will work for you?

That question focuses on the customer and probes for an open-ended response.

Let's look at some questions that have been developed by teams of salespeople in my seminars, and analyze them.

> Doesn't this seem to solve the issues we've been discussing?

Not a bad question. It puts the issue on the table, and asks for a positive response. It's open enough to give the customer some room to maneuver so that he doesn't necessarily feel manipulated. The "doesn't this..." is a bit manipulative, but it is probably acceptable in most situations.

? How does that fit for you? ?

I like this question. Again, it puts the issue on the table, but does so in an inquisitive tone that is open-ended and allows the customer to reflect.

? Where do we go from here? ?

Another candidate for my list of all-time best sales questions. This is assumptive in that it is built on the premise that "we" go. It asks the customer to identify the next step in her process. Once the customer responds, you merely have to nail down the date and time, and you have closed this portion of the sales process.

? What's the next step? ?

This is very similar to the previous question, and is one that can be used throughout the sales process. It's nonthreatening, and respects the customer and his buying process. This is less assumptive in that there is no hint of the "we go," as in the previous question; the customer can say something that has nothing to do with you. For example, your customer may respond, "I have to talk to your competitors and hear their proposals."

? Will our proposal meet the project schedule? ?

This question, presented by a seller of construction materials, is an attempt to gain a yes from the customer, and then build on that for a final request for an order. Under circumstances such that you know the answer is yes, it is probably an okay question.

? Are you going to need any other products for ? this project that aren't on the proposal?

This is a similar situation to the previous one. I think it is the wrong place for this question. It is basically a competence-creating question, in that it conveys to the customer the idea that the salesperson knows that there are often other products that aren't on the proposal. The salesperson, therefore, is experienced and knowledgeable about how business is done in this industry. But it causes the customer to lose focus by directing her thoughts to other issues. The real issue is the degree to which *your* proposal is right for this situation. It's probably not a better question for this situation.

? Tell me what you need. ?

Good question; wrong place. This is a great question to use prior to presenting your solution—not after. Remember where we are in the sales process: You have already discovered what your customer wanted, and have offered your solution. It may be that this question has an implied second part to it, and should be phrased this way:

? Tell me what you need in order to do this deal with me. ?

In that case, it is a better question, because it opens the dialogue up to a possible negotiation. The customer could say something such as: "Lower your price by 2 percent." You are now in a negotiation. That's a good place to be. You could then respond this way:

I'll have to check on that, because we have provided you a very competitive price. Tell me, if I'm able to lower the prices, would you then commit to buying the off-the-proposal add-ons from us?

The customer says yes or no, and you take it from there. Here's a better approach:

1. Summarize the key ways your solution meets the customer's specifications.
2. Use an open-ended, probing question to uncover the general sense of the customer's view of your solution.
3. If it is positive, nail down the next step. If it is negative, try to uncover the deeper issues.

Here's an example:

How does that seem to fit?

John replies, in a positive way: "Yeah, it looks pretty good." You nail down the next step.

The next step would probably be to bring a case in and try it. What do you think?

"Okay."

Easy. Simple.

Now, let's say the reply isn't positive. John says, in reply to your question, "I'm not sure it's right."

At this point, you have an objection, and you must successfully handle it. This challenge is a special sub-skill that is a part of the larger issue of gaining agreement with the customer.

An objection occurs when you ask a closing question such as, "Shall we go ahead?" and the customer says anything other than yes. For example, you ask if the customer is ready to go ahead, and she says, "No, I'm not ready to do that." Let's call that statement an objection.

Now what?

As always, a set of good questions is the best way to respond to an objection. My rule is: *First handle the person, and then deal with the content.*

Handling the person means that you understand that at the moment when your customers say no, that situation has changed dramatically. Now there is some tension in the relationship, as your customer has expressed a position in opposition to your perspective. The emotional atmosphere has changed. Your first objective is to diffuse the tension, and turn the conversation so that it is less about your differences and more about the two of you working together to uncover a solution.

First, empathize with the customer by making an statement such as this: "I can understand you feeling that way, John. It is a big decision." Tell the customer that you can understand what he is thinking or feeling, and give him a reason to believe you really do understand. Here's another example: "I can understand you thinking that, John; several of my other customers thought the same thing at first."

Your empathizing statement serves the function of diffusing the tension from the situation and conveying to the customer that you understand his point of view, and that it is okay for him to think or feel that way.

Now, follow up with an open-ended, probing question that digs into the customers position:

> ? Help me to understand. When you say you aren't ?
> . ready yet, what exactly does that mean? .

There are some other acceptable questions that can fit in this spot. For example, you could say,

? What makes you say that? ?

Or,

? Would you mind telling me why you said that? ?

Either way, you now need to listen proactively to the customer's response, dig a little deeper if you need to, and then verify her response with a closed-ended question:

? So, in other words, what you are saying is that you need to get the task force's approval before you can go ahead with the purchase. Is that right? ?

This is a great place, by the way, for a paraphrase.

At this point, if you have done your job properly and asked the right questions in the right sequence, your customer should respond with a yes. You've changed the atmosphere from confrontational to collaborative. Now you can address the content of the objection.

Once you have addressed the content, go back to where you started and pick up from there:

? What do you think? ?

You'll find your projects moving along at a faster pace, and considerably more of them turning into dollars. And that, after all, is the idea.

Questions to Help You Ensure Satisfaction

14

Too many salespeople consider the purchase order the final step in the sales process. Once they are awarded a purchase order, they are on to the next challenge. In so doing, they unknowingly neglect a sales call potentially rich in future potential. Following up on the sale is a powerful way to cement relationships and leverage the customer's feelings about the experience into future opportunities.

It is such a powerful sales call that I have a special name and format for it. I call it the PROF call. That acronym stands for the Problem-solving, Relationship-building, Opportunity-identifying, Follow-up call. And, yes, it does all of those things.

You use the PROF call after the customer has purchased something from you, the product or service has been delivered, and the customer has begun to implement it. It begins with a formal appointment to discuss the customer's experience. Make sure you let the customer know the purpose of the call. Because the product or service is new, it is on the customer's mind, and he generally won't mind talking with you about it. In fact, he is often favorably impressed that you would take the time to follow up.

Almost 15 years ago, I rented a small conference room from a local hotel. I just wanted to have a meeting of six of my clients for about 90 minutes. We bought soft drinks for all of them. It was probably the smallest sale the catering department of that hotel could make.

The day after the meeting, I received a call from the salesperson at the hotel, asking if everything was satisfactory. She inquired specifically about various aspects of the service, and wanted to make sure I was satisfied. I was impressed. For 15 years, I have told people that story, and mentioned the name of the hotel. It's been torn down now to make way for a new retail development, but for years, I sent people to that hotel based on the fact that the salesperson took the time to execute a PROF call with me.

Let's go back to how to implement a PROF call. First, make an appointment with the customer, and clearly identify the agenda for that appointment. Indicate that you want to follow up on the purchase, and explore other opportunities. Then, when you are in front of the customer, pursue these issues in this order: First, make sure the customer was satisfied with your product or service. A simple, open-ended question will usually do the trick:

> How are you doing with [the name of your product or service]?

If there is a problem, now is the time to discover it, apologize, and do what you can to fix it. If not, and the customer indicates that it is going well, then you confirm it with a closed-ended question such as:

? So, you are satisfied with what you bought from us? ?

This should prompt the customer to say yes. That verbalized affirmation is something upon which you can then build.

Now, move on to the next stage. Once you have ascertained that the customer is satisfied with the product, probe his experience with your company. Say something along these lines:

? And was everything okay with your experiences with the company in general? No problems with the delivery, the invoice was correct, and so on? ?

Once again, your strategy is to uncover any issues of dissatisfaction and try to resolve them, in the same way you did with the previous question. If the customer raises some issue as a result of this question, apologize, and tell him you'll do what you can to fix the situation. If he answers in any way you interpret as being satisfied, then, once again, try to confirm that with a closed-ended statement:

? Sounds like the whole experience was pretty satisfactory. ?

What you are trying to do is prompt the customer to verbalize an affirmative response.

Now that you have that affirmative, you can proceed to the next step, which is to build on the affirmative and probe for other opportunities. Think in terms of two types of opportunities: internal and external. *Internal* means other opportunities for your products or services within this account. Follow up the customer's affirmative reply with what is a natural, logical next step:

> ? Great. I'm glad everything worked well. What other issues ?
>   do you have with which we might be able to help you?

Use whatever variation on this question fits your unique situation. For example, if you sell construction materials or services, substitute "projects" for "issues."

If the customer offers some opportunity, then you revert to the questions that help you understand what they want. (Chapters 9, 10, and 11.)

If the customer has nothing for you, then hang in there for one more step. Remember: At this point, he has said he is satisfied with you and your company twice. Two yeses. So probe for some external opportunities—referrals to other companies or other decision-makers within his organization. Ask something similar to this:

> ? What other departments or people within ?
>   the organization could use what we do?

Or,

> ? To what other companies like yours would you refer me? ?

If you receive any positive answer to either of these two questions, then nail it down with a phone number if possible, and a commitment from the customer to allow you to use his name in contacting the other company. At that point, you have leveraged the satisfaction to wring the greatest value out of the event.

Clearly, the PROF call is a powerful way to get more value out of a recent satisfactory purchase.

There is another even more common situation that falls into this category. It is one of the most common situations for business-to-business sellers, but one that is rarely addressed by sales trainers. In this situation, you have an existing relationship with the customer, and the customer is buying something from you. The customer has far greater potential to buy other products or services from you. That means that you have a position of some trust in the account, and the customer has taken some risk with you; you are now the low-risk choice. The challenge is to leverage your current relationship in order to uncover other opportunities for your goods and services.

Once again, the well-phrased, appropriately asked question is the key. Here is a series of questions developed by salespeople in my seminars for this specific application, with my comments following.

? What has to change for us to do more business here? ?

This is another of my nominees for the all-time best sales questions. It can be used a couple of times a year in those accounts in which there is a lot of additional potential, but in which you seem to be stymied. I chanced upon this question in just such an account; it had huge potential, but after 18 months of fruitless effort, I was getting nowhere. Out of frustration, I asked this question. I remember the answer word for word:

"It's nothing about you, Dave. But you know, we've been doing business with your competitor for a whole lot longer than you have been around. He takes very good care of us. As long as he's here, we're going to do most of our business with him. Now, if that should ever change, it would be a different situation."

I thanked the customer for his candor, reduced the time I spent in that account, and waited patiently for things to change. Six months later, the salesperson to whom they had been so loyal was promoted out of the territory, and I had my chance. Three years after that, it had become my biggest account. I attribute my success to the question I asked. Ask it at least twice a year. The answer customers give you in June may be different than the answer they give you in January.

? What can we do to earn more of your business? ?

I don't like this question nearly as well. The emphasis is on you, when in fact it may not be at all about you, as in my previous example.

This question also provides the customer with the option to interject responses that may introduce a negative element into the relationship. It may be, for example, that she will answer with something that you cannot possibly do. She could say, "Deliver three times a week on your own truck." You use common carriers to deliver your goods, so the customer's request is out of the question. You have put yourself in a position of having to say to the customer that you cannot do what she asked you to do. So you have surfaced and given substance to an issue that can now stand in your way of your further penetrating the account.

? Is your company prepared to invest in a comprehensive vendor-managed inventory? ?

In this case, the supplier is advocating a vendor-managed inventory program to the customer, and is using this question as a lead-in to a discussion of the benefits of such a program. However, because it is a closed-ended question, the salesperson is taking a risk that the customer will answer in a negative way. For example, if the customer says no, then the salesperson's entire approach is down the drain. He has no right to start discussing the program when the customer has already said he's not interested. As we've seen in earlier questions, it is better not to force the customer to voice a negative position. This question is better left unasked.

Instead, think of using this more open variation:

? What are your thoughts on a comprehensive vendor-managed inventory program? ?

The customer may still say, "We have no interest." But your question didn't force her into voicing that position. Your question gave the customer latitude to share ideas and values with you that could potentially be built upon to lead up to a presentation of her system.

> Is there anything else besides price that would convince you to change?

This is a terrible question. It's a closed-ended question that forces the customer to voice a position. If he says no, then you are reduced to dealing on price, and the customer has you in a position such that the only thing you can come back on is a discounted price. This is another example of behaviors and questions of salespeople that often cause us to default to a discounted price.

If he says yes, then you must, of course, follow up with, "What's that?" The customer then may say something that appeals to your strengths, but is just as likely to want something you can't possibly do. He may say, for example, "Repackage all your products into procedure-based kits." Your company can't possibly do that. So your question, once again, prompted the customer to take a position that rules you out. What possible reason would you have for ever again visiting this customer when he's told you that? Your poor question locked you out of the account.

> How is [your product] working out for you?

Nice question. It's open-ended, nonthreatening, and genuinely inquisitive of the customer's satisfaction.

> How can we broaden our spectrum of services?

I'm undecided about this question. On one hand, I believe it is our job as salespeople to show the customer how we can broaden our products or services. In that sense, the question is a bit unfair. On the other hand, if you have a great relationship with the customer, she may answer this in a way that will be helpful to you. Then again, if you had that kind of relationship, you'd probably be doing most of the business, and wouldn't need to ask this question.

> ? Would a new and unique product ?
>   be an advantage to you?

Bad question. There you go again asking a closed-ended question that may prompt the customer to verbalize a position that closes you down. What do you do if he says no? Excuse yourself and hope he'll see you again sometime in the future.

> ? Who are your current suppliers, and ?
>   why did you choose them?

I can't imagine that a group of five or six experienced sales-people, putting their heads together and brainstorming questions for this situation, could possibly have come up with this one. It is one of the worst questions I can imagine.

First of all, what are you going to prompt the customer to think about? All your competitors, and why she does business with them and not you. Not only is she going to think about them, she's going to tell you about them, lending the power of a publicly held position to the mix. So you've just made the only way to gain more business in this account to get the customer to back down from her position. Talk about making your job more difficult.

Secondly, it shows, by its focus, that you are more interested in your competitors than you are in this customer. This question has nothing to do with the customer; it has to do with your competitors. What possible good can come of it? Horrible question.

Here's a better way: Begin by identifying the company's goals, move on to identifying some aspect of the business that is lagging behind, and then zero in the opportunities for your company in that area.

Here's an example: Let's say you are selling janitorial supplies—all the stuff the company uses to clean its facilities. You are selling hand soap and hand towels for the restrooms, but you know that you could also be supplying the soaps and waxes they use on their floors.

You start out with something similar to this:

> Where do you anticipate the organization is headed in the next few years?

The customer responds with a discussion of the organization's growth plans and the need to become more profitable. You decide to build upon the "more profitable" comment.

> Are there plans in place to increase your profitability?

This is a closed-ended question, but it doesn't make any difference to you which way the customer answers. If he says yes, you probe into that and piggyback your solution onto one of the plans. If he says, no, you suggest your solution as a way to reach the goal of greater profitability.

In this case, let's say the customer says yes, and talks about one of the initiatives to reduce overall labor costs. This is exactly the opening for which you have been looking. You say:

"That's a situation just made for our solutions. We have some cleaning products for your floors that can reduce the amount of labor your people spend at this routine task. We could make you look like a hero. Tell me, who should I see to arrange for a discussion of this?"

By using open-ended, probing questions, and starting with the organization's goals, you have uncovered an opportunity for additional products, and moved one step closer to your goal of further penetrating this account. That is a better way to open up additional opportunities and achieve success at this stage of the sales process.

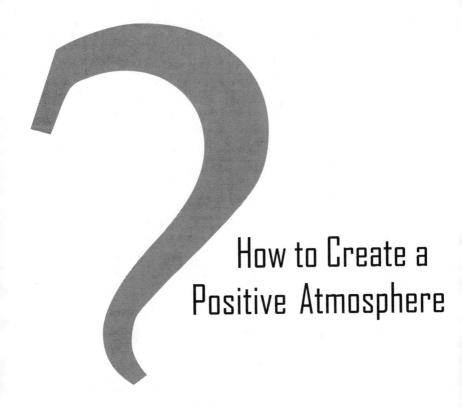

How to Create a
Positive Atmosphere

15 No matter how well you have prepared your questions, if the customer isn't comfortable with you or doesn't trust you, he's not going to answer your questions thoroughly and honestly. All of your hard work in creating better questions would be for nothing. So, if you are going to use questions effectively, you must master another element—creating an emotional atmosphere surrounding your engagement with the customer that is conducive to him answering your questions thoroughly and honestly.

There always is an emotional atmosphere. Even though we may sometimes like to think that the sales decision is all intellectual—all about the suitability of your solution to the customer's needs—the truth is that almost everyone feels something about everyone they meet. How your customers feel about you and your company is a major part of every sale.

Your customers feel something about you. Those feelings may not be intense, and they may not be at the surface of their minds, but they are still there. Sometimes a negative emotion can derail all your efforts to capture a sale.

Here's an example from my life. A few years ago, I came to realize that my neighbor's yard was much greener and fuller than mine, and I felt bad about the wimpy look of my yard. So I determined to use the same company he used to fertilize his yard.

I called the company with the intention of buying. The salesperson answered my questions and set up a date for the first application. I asked him to have the technician drop off some literature on the various programs and options, and after reading it, I would decide which program I wanted. I'm a visual guy. I like to read things—particularly if money is involved. He said, okay, they would do that, and that I could cancel the service at any time with 30 days notice. I said, "Excuse me, I'm not signing up for an extended program right now. So there's nothing to cancel."

He said he understood, but that they only signed people up for a program. I told him that wasn't what I wanted. I got a suspicious feeling about him. First he had indicated that I could do just one application, and then he said I would need to sign up for a "program" that I could "cancel at anytime with 30 days notice." I didn't believe him.

He said, "Yes, but...."

I said, "Never mind, I'll go elsewhere." And I hung up.

Looking back on it, the reason I hung up is because I had an emotional reaction to the salesperson. He contradicted himself. As a result, I didn't trust him. And because I didn't trust him, I wasn't going to do business with him. Believe me, there are dozens of companies who could provide a similar service. My decision had nothing to do with the quality of the service, the price, or anything else. It all had to do with my emotional reaction to the salesperson.

Now that may have been a bit dramatic, but the moral of the story applies to every sales call we make. We have an emotional effect on the customer; he feels something about us. And, if we disregard that emotional impact, we can render all of our well-designed questions useless.

In my sales seminars, I often teach the competency of creating rapport and building relationships just before we address the competency of asking good sales questions. There's a reason for that. The state of the relationship has a direct effect on the salesperson's ability to have the customer answer his or her questions honestly and thoroughly. If the customer is comfortable with you, knows you, and trusts you, he will generally share deep and detailed information with you. The opposite is also true. If he doesn't trust you, he's not going to be candid with you.

The competency of building relationships with the customer is a much larger issue than is within the scope of this book. It may be a future book. For now, I want to focus on those things you can do in the sales call to create rapport with the customer.

Create Rapport

Here's the dictionary definition of *rapport*: "An emotional bond or friendly relationship between people based on mutual liking, trust and a sense that they understand and share each other's concerns."

Unlike a relationship, which takes time, rapport can be instant. Although it can be a part of a relationship, and with time can evolve into a positive business relationship, it can also stand by itself. You don't need to have a deep relationship with a person in order to have rapport with him.

Rapport just makes it so much easier for customers to be honest and thorough with you. If they feel an emotional bond with you, if they feel that you understand each other, if they feel that you share their concerns, they will be much more likely to open up to you.

Rapport, among the general population, often happens spontaneously. It is not unusual for a person to just feel comfortable with someone without necessarily trying. But a salesperson is a professional, and understands that the ability to create rapport with the customer, to make the customer feel comfortable, is a desirable thing to create, and is much too important to be left to chance. A professional salesperson studies how rapport is achieved, and with discipline and willfulness puts into practice the things that will make a customer feel rapport with us.

Here are eight specific practices that will build rapport with another person. Which you use depends on your reading of the other person and your own set of strengths. Pick and choose those that most resonate with you.

1. Appearance

You should look as similar to the other person as possible. That doesn't mean that you have a set of wigs in the car and put on the one that matches the hair color and style of your customer. But it does mean that you look as though you are of the same "class" of person as the customer. That doesn't necessarily mean economic class; it's a larger term than just that. If you are calling on executives, for example, you should look the way an executive would. If you are calling on restaurant owners, you should look as though you are of that group. Study your customers and find things that characterize this group of people. As you do, methodically put them into your routines.

Pay attention to your dress. My rule has always been this: Dress like your customers, only a little better.

Your dress should convey to the customer that you are similar to her, not different from her. There was a time when men in a suit and tie and women in a skirted suit was the expected mode of dress. However, if you are calling on maintenance supervisors, foreman, or uniformed personnel, that dress separates you from your customer, making you seem aloof and unapproachable.

So, how does your customer dress?

One of my clients sold supplies to farmers. Dressing in flannel shirts, blue jeans, and boots was okay, because that was how the farmers dressed. But note the second part of the rule: "a little better." That's where your positioning as a successful, competent person comes in. You should, within the context of the customer's world, look successful, competent, and confident. So, if you are going to wear jeans and flannel shirts, they should be good quality jeans (a good brand name), clean, and pressed. Your flannel shirt should be a better-than-average brand, clean, and pressed.

If you are calling on management-level people, it gets a little more challenging. In today's world, some companies adhere to a coat-and-tie discipline, whereas others prescribe "business casual" for their employees. Honestly, I keep notes in my customer files as to what the mode of dress is in that organization. I keep it simple by using two categories: C&T (coat & tie), and BC (business casual). When I'm making one of my rare face-to-face sales calls, I check the file the day before so that I know how to dress.

One of the salespeople in one of my classes shared his approach with me. He explained that he always wore gray dress slacks, a light blue button-down collared shirt, a tie, and a navy blazer. That way, he could dress up or down, depending on the situation. With the tie and blazer, he felt comfortable calling on coat-and-tie executives. If the call required a conversation with a front-line supervisor, he'd remove the tie, and leave the blazer in the car. A nice approach. I'm sure there is a similar outfit that can be spontaneously dressed up or down for women as well.

2. Disarming honesty

Many of our daily conversations are composed of predict-able responses to predictable statements. If you break out of the mold and answer a question or response to a statement with disarming honesty instead of expected formality, it often breaks through barriers and helps establish immediate rapport. For example, when someone says, "How are you?" I will some-times say something such as this: "Honestly, I'm a bit tired. Had a busy weekend and it's hard to get going on a Monday." Quite often my customer will respond to this bit of disarming honesty with something similar to this: "I know what you mean. I did not want to get out of bed this morning."

There, we've achieved a bit of mutual understanding and shared concerns—the definition of rapport.

3. Humor

If you are one of those fortunate people who have the abil-ity to make people laugh, it is a great gift that can be a powerful rapport builder. When someone laughs with you, the barriers come down, and a certain unspoken emotional bond takes their place.

I, unfortunately, am not very good at this. I learned a long time ago that I should not tell jokes. Too often, I forget the punch line. And even when I remember it, the joke is never as funny when I tell it as when I heard it. This is one of those practices that is powerful in the hands of those with the ability, and disaster for those without.

4. Sincere compliment

I'm amazed at how infrequently people are complimented. It must be for that reason that so many people are noticeably and positively affected by a sincere compliment. It doesn't have to be grandiose, and should not, of course, seem contrived. But a sincere compliment for something you have noticed about the person, his office, his environment, or his business, can go a long way to making people feel good about you.

5. Perceptive question

This is a variation of the complement. If you notice something somewhat unique or distinctive about the customer or her organization, ask a question about it. Remember all of the things a good sales question does: It makes the person feel important, shows your interest, and provides her with something to talk about.

You may, for example, say something similar to this (a question I recently asked on a first call with a prospect):

> This building has such a good, comfortable feel to it. Did you intend that when you were building it?

That, of course, led to a discussion of the feel of the building, and what the company was trying to achieve in the design and decoration of it. It made the customer feel that I understood him, and that we shared at least this one thing in common. And that, of course, is the definition of rapport.

6. Reflective behavior

This is too big an issue to give justice to in this small space. It basically describes the incredibly powerful technique of reflecting your customer's communication style. If your customer is direct and to the point, for example, you can use language that is direct and to the point. If your customer is soft and fluffy and people-oriented, you can use that style in talking with her. As you reflect the customer's style back to her, you send a powerful subconscious message that you are just like her. Your customer then feels more comfortable with you.

7. Personal connection

? Yeah, I was there on vacation too. Did you have a chance to visit the [attraction] while you were there? ?

Boom. A connection made as two people who both had the same experience. In this case, a place we had both been on vacation. The more things such as this you have in common, the more your customer feels rapport with you. So, actively seek to uncover and express anything and everything you may have in common with your customer.

8. Personal story

This doesn't have to be a long, drawn-out narrative. Even a few words about something you experienced, a problem you had, or a positive moment in your life can do the trick. It just means that you take the initiative to tell a personal story. In so doing, you toss out to the customer an experience to which he may be able to relate. If so, good, you've achieved some rapport.

Here's an example: You've just said hello to your customer. Before another word is said, you jump into the conversation with something similar to this: "Boy, I almost got broadsided on my way into the parking lot. A guy was so busy talking on his cell phone that he didn't even notice the stop sign and rolled right on through. I'm lucky to be here."

There probably isn't a customer in the world who can't relate to that experience. The customer may say something such as, "Yeah, I know what you mean. They should outlaw talking on cell phone when you drive." Guess what? You've just achieved a mutual understanding, a shared experience, a value you both share. That's rapport.

In the hands of a professional salesperson, these practices serve to create rapport with almost anyone. And that means that the customer is much more likely to share honestly and thoroughly with you.

Law of Reciprocity

Beyond rapport, are there things you can do to encourage and generate an emotional atmosphere that is conducive to the customer answering your questions? Of course.

Let's begin by identifying the kind of atmosphere we want. If you were to describe the ideal atmosphere that characterizes the relationship between you and your customer in this particular sales call, I expect that you would use words such as *comfortable, honest, thorough,* and *concerned.* If I was tagging along with you, and registered my observations of the emotions the customer was feeling, hopefully I would describe them in those words.

So, if that comprises the ideal emotional environment, what can you do to encourage and stimulate those emotions?

The single most powerful principle and set of practices to accomplish are wrapped up in a concept I call the "Law of Reciprocity." The Law of Reciprocity is an observation of human nature. It says, "generally speaking, people will react to you emotionally in the way in which you first act toward them."

We instinctively know this to be true, but we rarely consider it as a strategy in our sales interactions. For example, if you walk down the street and look an oncoming pedestrian in the eye and give her a nice, warm smile, the most likely thing to have happen is she will smile back. This is the Law of Reciprocity at work.

It can work in a negative way as well. Let's say you have had a miserable day. You got kicked out of a major account, got a flat tire, and stepped in a mud puddle up to your knee. So you come in the house and slam the door shut, and throw your briefcase down. Does your spouse approach you and say, "Oh, honey, it's so nice to have you home"? Not in my house. If I came in that way, my wife would more than likely respond in kind, with a grumpy, "What's wrong with you?"

The emotions we project are the emotions that are reflected back to us. It's why negative people often find themselves in a self-fulfilling prophecy, surrounded by other negative people. They projected negativity, and it came back at them. Positive people, on the other hand, have every reason to remain positive, surrounded, as they are, by so many other positive people—a result of their subtle influencing of the world around them.

Now, understanding the Law of Reciprocity, we can use the principle to influence our sales behavior. If we are intent on encouraging some emotions, we must *be first* that which we want our customers to be.

- If we want our customers to be comfortable with us, we must first be comfortable with them.
- If we want our customers to be honest with us, we must first be honest with them.
- If we want our customers to be thorough with us, we must first be thorough with them.
- If we want our customers to be concerned with us, we must first be concerned with them.

The Law of Reciprocity, consistently applied, will subtly influence the emotional atmosphere of your sales interactions, encouraging your customers to share more and deeper information with you.

Making your customer comfortable with you is an essential step in every sales process. Without that, the answers to your questions will not be as accurate and thorough as you'd like them to be. It's an essential part of asking questions effectively.

How to Listen
Constructively

16 If you do everything I've described so far, and yet you miss the details and intricacies contained in your customer's answers, it has all been a waste of time. The thoughts your questions have created— and the words they gave birth to--are the very reason for your questions. That means that you must focus on capturing the information in those words. And that means you need to listen constructively—with more discipline and method than ever before.

It sounds so simple. We can all listen. Yet we don't listen as well as we should or could. Remember the discussion of the traits of the superstars from Chapter 1?

The superstar salespeople could see the situation from the customer's point of view because they asked "better questions" and "listened more constructively."

It seems that "listening constructively" is so rare, it is one of the ways the superstars vault themselves to higher levels than the average salesperson. There's a lesson in that for us. We can, and should, listen better than we do.

It's easy enough to understand why listening is so difficult for all of us. It has to do with our minds' ability to think far more rapidly than we can speak. Our minds can think, according to researchers, at something around 1000–1200 words per minute. We can speak, on the other hand, at most, at about 200 words per minute.

So, what happens is that our minds race ahead of the words our customer says, causing a gap in our ability to listen. We just naturally think more rapidly than they talk, and so we fill the gap with non-listening kinds of thoughts. In order to overcome this natural imbalance, we need to focus our resources on the task. Listening well takes discipline, willfulness, and commitment.

Constructive listening

Constructive listening is a specific type of listening for salespeople. My wife is a crisis counselor, and talks about listening empathetically. But empathetic listening isn't really advocated for salespeople. Constructive listening requires the salesperson to listen for things upon which to build—to build his response, the next question, the proposal, and so on.

Good listening—constructive listening—has an incredibly powerful effect on the quality of the sales interaction. We tend to view it as one-sided, in that, by listening constructively, we gain more information from the customer. The focus is on us. However, it sends powerful messages to the customer, and affects him as well.

If you are a good listener, for example, you send the message that:

- You are interested in the other person.
- You are willing to hold back on your agenda, in deference to the customer's.
- You are flexible.
- You respect the other person.
- You can separate the person from the problem.

All of these are good things for the customer to realize about you. And the single most powerful way you create these perceptions in the customer's mind to listen better and more constructively than ever before.

Unfortunately, most salespeople are terrible at this crucial skill. Perhaps that is because of some common misperceptions of what effective sales is all about. Have you ever heard the expression, "He has the gift of gab"? That implies that talking is the ultimate sales skill. Or maybe you've heard of the "fast-talking salesperson," which again implies that salespeople talk more than they listen.

As a check on your current practice, here's a list of the most common negative listening habits in which salespeople too often engage. Compare your practices to this list.

1. You do all the talking.
2. You interrupt when other people talk.
3. You never look at the person to indicate you are listening.
4. You start to argue or interrupt before the other person has a chance to finish.
5. Everything that is said reminds you of an experience you have had, and you feel obligated to digress with a story.
6. You finish sentences for people if they pause too long.

7. You wait with obvious impatience for people to
    finish so that you can interject something.

These may be the most obvious listening faults. Regardless, every one of us can improve our ability to listen constructively. Here are a number of ways to improve your ability to
listen constructively.

1. Manage the acoustic climate.

This may seem obvious. The first requirement of listening
constructively is accurately hearing what your customer says.
If you can't hear, accurately and completely, then you can't
listen.

This means that, when you are in a situation in which you
may have trouble hearing, you have to be assertive and try and
change the situation. For example, if you're trying to have a
conversation on a noisy production floor, say to the customer:

? Do you mind if we go into the lunch room to talk? **?**

Or, if people are continually interrupting, ask the customer
if you can close the door or put the phone on hold. If you're on
the phone and experiencing difficulty, ask to call back on a
better line, or ask her to move to a quieter phone.

If you are polite and ask, most people are happy to comply.
If they don't, then at least you tried.

2. Implant questions in your mind.

Have you ever taken a speed-reading course? If so, you'll
recognize one of the techniques you are taught. When you
want to speed-read a book, you first look at the table of con-
tents, and ask yourself questions about each chapter. Things
such as:

? I wonder what the author's main point is. **?**

? What information does he use to support that? ?

? What does he claim to be some of ?
    the implications of his idea?

Just as a good question directs our customer's thinking, so too we can use a series of good questions to direct our conscious and subconscious thinking. When you place these questions in your mind, your subconscious mind will seek for the answers. You can take in whole blocks of text at a time, and your subconscious will sift through them, attempting to find the answers to your questions. This technique, which is proven as a powerful speed-reading device, can also be used to improve your listening ability.

Before every sales call, take a few moments to ask yourself the questions for which you want the answers. Implant them into your mind in the same way you do when you are speed reading. Then, expect your subconscious to seek the answers. Instead of reading for them, you'll be listening for them.

3. Listen to more than just words.

We've all heard that a greater part of a person's communication comes through his body language rather than the words he chooses to use. I'm not sure I believe that. Regardless of how much communication is contained in the body language and how much in the words, the fact is that words are always embellished, and given perspective, by nonverbal communication.

To focus only on the words, and thus to ignore the signs and signals coming though a person's nonverbal communication, is to be extremely limited in our understanding of what the person is thinking and feeling.

Good listeners, then, listen for more than just words. Be sensitive to the tone of voice that accompanies each response.

Watch the customer's body language. Here's a table of the most common nonverbal signs and what they mean.

Reading Nonverbal Communication

If you see this:	Your customer probably is:
Arms raised on chest; fist clenched; arms gripped; pointing index finger	Defensive
Head tilted; peering over glasses; cleaning glasses; stroking chin; glasses in mouth	Reflective/Evaluating
Open hands; uncrossing legs; unbuttoning coat	Open
Leaning forward; hand supporting chin; sitting on edge of chair	Interested
Rubbing eyes; rubbing nose; rubbing next to ear; squirming in chair	Suspicious
Clearing throat; cigarette smoking; fidgeting in chair; jingling coins in pocket; rubbing palm on clothes; chewing pencil; playing with hair; poor eye contact	Nervous
Sitting on edge of chair; standing with hands on hip	Ready

Erect stance; frequent eye contact held longer; hands joined together at back; hands on lapels; steepled hands	Confident
Fingers drumming; toes tapping; pen clicking; eyes dropping; deep breath; glazed eyes; rubbing palms or fingers or thumb of same hand	Bored
Hands to chest, hands spread palm out	Expecting
Eyes focused straight ahead	Receiving information
Eyes positioned upward and to the right	Relating to a personal experience
Eyes positioned upward and to the left	Relating to the past with more intense involvement
Eyes cast downward	Emotionally involved

4. Take notes.

This is where some of those skills from your days in school will actually come into play. You should always have a pad of paper and a writing instrument when you are talking to a customer. You should always take notes.

Not only does that force you to listen to the customer, but it also says to him that what he is saying is so important, you want to write it down. That's a powerful and positive message to send to the customer.

Your notes should focus on "things to build upon." What did the customer say that you deem important, understanding your agenda and where you want the conversation to go? If the customer says anything such as, "The real problem is..." or "the bottom line is..." you'll want to capture those thoughts word for word.

You should also make notes of any unique language or figures of speech the customer uses. You'll want to use those when it is time to talk to her, as the best salespeople always use the customer's language, not their own.

5. Respond positively.

It's normal to think that the sequence of events in a conversation with your customer should go this way: You ask a question, your customer answers, and then you ask another question.

I'd recommend that you follow a slightly different sequence: You ask a question, your customer answers, you respond to the customer's answer, and then you ask your next question.

I recommend a communication intervention called a *response*. What's a response?

A response is a verbal or nonverbal signal you give to the customer that says to him, in effect, "See, I'm listening. I'm striving to understand. I'm accepting what you are saying."

When you master the use of effective responses, you subtly and psychologically reward the customer for answering your question, and you make it much more likely that he will continue to answer your questions with candor and thoroughness.

Here are some responses:

1. Short verbal prompts.

Use short, verbal interjections following the customer's answer. Things like "Oh?" "Really," "Okay," and "Thanks." When you follow the customer's answer with one of these short responses, you send her the message that you are listening and focusing on her.

Here's a powerful technique that will vault you into the major leagues of listeners. When you ask the customer a question, listen to his answer. Then, pick one or two words out of the customer's answer, and repeat them back to him, nodding your head. It is even more powerful if you pick out the one or two most important words he said.

Here's an example: You ask a question such as,

> What are some of the challenges that have you most concerned these days?

Your customer explains that she is responsible for making sure that sufficient inventories of parts are continuously on hand so that the production lines stay in continuous operation. She remarks that she's concerned that the recent publicity over defective products from overseas may be true for some of the items she is purchasing. A few defective parts could shut down the production lines, and cause her all kinds of problems.

You say, "Defective parts," and nod your head.

That's it. Nothing too strenuous. But in so doing you send the powerful message to the customer that you have listened, captured the essence of what she said to you, and subtly reward her for answering. And, of course, this little technique forces you to listen for the one or two key words in the customer's answer.

2. Paraphrase.

This is very similar to the one- or two-word technique just described, yet is much more intense. The process is the same—you listen carefully to what the customer is saying. Then, instead of just repeating one or two words, you paraphrase the customer's response in your own words, repeat that back to him, and ask him if you have understood him correctly.

Here's an example: You ask your customer this question:

> To what degree do you feel that you have the issue of defective parts under control?

Your customer says, "I wish I did. I'm just not comfortable with some of the suppliers we have been using in recent years. I know that they import many of their components from overseas, and we have never had an opportunity to examine their quality procedures. Having said that, I have to say that as of today, we've had no real problems."

You say,

> Let me see if I understand you correctly. In other words, you are concerned about what might be a lack of QC in some of your suppliers, but at the moment, you haven't yet experienced any real problem. Is that right?

Your customer may say yes. That, of course, confirms that you have understood him correctly. Or it could be that you didn't get everything he wanted to say, in which case he'll say something such as "Not exactly," and then go on to explain further.

In either case, the outcome is positive. In the first instance, he's confirmed that you have understood him correctly. That's a good thing.

In the second case, he knows that you are working at understanding him, and is going to explain further and provide you with more information. That's a good thing as well.

When you commit to use either or both of these techniques, you'll find that they work just as powerfully in you as they do to influence the customer. Because you commit to paraphrase or summarize and repeat, that action focuses you to listen more constructively. So, they are self-management tactics that raise your listening acumen at the same time that they prompt the customer to share more information.

Listening, and listening ever more constructively, is one of the key skills for a salesperson. What you hear from the customer is, ultimately, the reason for all your work at questioning. It deserves just as much of your effort.

More Questions
to Ask Yourself

17 In the first chapter, I proposed two basic sets of questions with which a dedicated salesperson should gain competence: Questions to ask prospects and customers, and questions to ask yourself. Most of this book has been devoted to questions of prospects and customers, but that doesn't mean those questions are any more important than those we ask ourselves.

Questions we ask ourselves are just as—if not more—important as those we ask our prospects and customers. The reason goes back to the ultimate power of a question— it directs our thinking. Just as a good question directs the customer's thinking, so too does a good question direct our own thinking. And thinking well is the ultimate success skill for a professional salesperson.

Some years ago, I was interviewing a group of salespeople for a consulting project in which I was engaged. One of the salespeople, upon reflection, said, "I've come to realize that sales is really a thinking person's game."

I couldn't agree more. Ultimately, the way you bring greater results into your organization, make an outstanding career for yourself, and provide more abundantly for your family, is by outthinking your peers and your competitors. Thinking—good thinking done with discipline and methodology—is the ultimate competitive skill.

Yet few salespeople, and few people in general, regularly engage in good thinking. As the philosopher Bertrand Russell said, "Most people would rather die than think. In fact, they do."

This chapter is not designed to be the final word on how salespeople could think more effectively (that's the next book!). However, there are some easily applied rules, processes and practices that will enable you to *think better* and dramatically affect your performance.

Let's start with a simple definition of good thinking for a salesperson: *Good thinking is asking yourself the right questions, in the right sequence, at the right times, and writing down the answers.*

It sounds so simple, and it is. The power, as with so much in the world of the salesperson, is in the excellent and disciplined execution. The rest of this chapter is going to discuss what it means to ask yourself the right questions, in the right sequence, at the right times, but at this point I want to make the case for writing down the answers.

"Writing down," either as typing on a computer or handwriting on a pad of paper, is one of the disciplines of good thinking. The very act of writing focuses you on the exact words that formulate your answers. You can be vague and indistinct as long as the answer is just something you maintain in your mind, but when you force yourself to write the answers down you must select the exact words that go on paper. Thus, writing is a discipline that forces you to think precisely—one of the tenets of good thinking.

Secondly, putting it in print is an act of commitment. Once you've written the answer, it is there for you to review forever. Not only does it serve as a commitment—after all, *you* wrote it—but it is also a reminder that you have already gone down this path before and come up with an answer. When you confront the question that prompted that answer again, you'll save time by referring to your previous work.

So, if you are going to think well, you'll write the answers to your questions down on paper.

What, then, are some of the "right questions" to ask yourself? I've organized them into two major categories: Personal Effectiveness Questions, and Personal Improvement Questions.

Personal Effectiveness Questions

There is a set of questions so powerful, they have more to do with the eventual success of a salesperson than any other single issue. The questions, or, more appropriately, the answers to those questions, are so important that the best salespeople develop disciplines and methods to consistently answer those questions as effectively as possible.

What are the questions?

? Where do I go? ?

? Who do I see? ?

? What should I do? ?

Almost every field salesperson has the freedom to ask and answer those questions continuously in the course of the day. We ask and answer them moment by moment, hour by hour, day by day, week by week, and month by month. If you can consistently develop the most effective answers to these questions, you will put yourself in a position to be one of the outstanding salespeople in your industry. If you default to answering these questions by habit, by being reactive, or by other mindless methods, you detract from your success. The effective answers to these questions put you in front of the right people, and keep you focused on the most effective things to do. And that is a prescription for success.

Annual thinking and planning retreat

In order to answer these three questions over and over again in the most effective way, you must do some additional work. That includes dedicating specific chunks of time to thinking disciplines. For example, you need to invest in an annual "thinking and planning" retreat, where you take a day or two and thoroughly think through the upcoming year, asking and answering specific questions. One set of those annual questions includes these:

> Which of my accounts holds the greatest potential for sales growth this year?

The answer to this question should lead you to three categories of customers/prospects: A, B, and C. The "A" list, identified by potential for growth, is the ultimate answer to this question. (For greater detail on this issue, see Chapter 4 of my book *10 Secrets of Time Management for Salespeople.*)

> What do I want to accomplish this year, personally as well as professionally?

It can take you half a day to answer this question with depth and detail. The answers, of course, form your goals for the year. You ought to have personal goals as well as professional or sales goals for the coming year. For example, do you want to lose 20 pounds? Improve your relationship with your teenagers? Become more spiritual? These kinds of answers comprise the raw material for your personal goals.

> **? What would you like to produce in terms of total sales? How many new customers? How much in key product line sales? ?**

These kinds of sub-questions are ways you think more precisely about what you want to achieve professionally, and again, form the raw material for your sales goals.

Finally, at your annual "thinking and planning" retreat, you ought to answer this question with respect to each of the goals your prior questions and answers produced:

> **? What is the best way to accomplish each of these? ?**

Notice the sequence: First we asked what we wanted to accomplish, and then we asked what was the best way to do so. Good thinking is asking the right questions, in the right sequence, at the right times. Your answer to that question could be a paragraph or two, or maybe even one side of one page of paper, for each of the goals you created by asking the earlier questions.

When you have finished this annual exercise in thinking and planning, you will have a set of answers that will guide your decisions each day, each week, and each month.

Monthly planning session

In the world of the professional B2B salesperson, it is so easy to become immersed in the frenzied activity that often describes our days that we lose track of the commitments we made. We create the answers to the questions in our annual thinking and planning retreat, and then, two months later, discover we are so overwhelmed by the pressure of everyday stuff, we haven't given our commitments any thought.

It is for that reason that we need to establish a discipline of reviewing and refining our thinking each and every month. A monthly planning session is an opportunity to stop, take a deep breath, and refocus on those things we previously determined were the most important. Without that monthly discipline, we risk being knocked off-course.

A monthly planning session should be an investment of one to two hours, once a month, at about the same time each month. In it, you ask yourself these questions, and answer them in writing:

? Last month, did I do what I said I was going to do? ?

? If not, why not? ?

? What should I do differently this month? ?

Having reviewed your previous month's performance, you now must plan for the most effective use of your time for the coming month. That means you ask, and answer in writing, these questions:

? What are the most important things I want to accomplish this month? ?

? What specific progress do I want to make in my target accounts? ?

? What specific progress do I want to make ?
in selling key products or lines?

? What specific deals do I want to close this month? ?

? What specific progress do I want to make ?
in acquiring new customers?

? How am I going to improve myself this month? ?

It can take an hour or two to develop written answers to these questions. The resulting document is, however, your best thinking about the most effective things you can do this month. Use it to guide your day-to-day decisions; you'll become far more effective, just because you regularly think with discipline and method.

Weekly planning

Dedicate an hour or two once a week to the task of getting thoroughly prepared for the coming week. The questions you ask and answer here are becoming ever more specific:

? Where do I want to go each day this week? ?

? What do I want to accomplish by the end of the week? ?

? What do I need in order to do so? ?

As a result of asking and answering these questions, you'll find yourself assembling the literature, samples, price quotes, and so on that you need, with plenty of time to spare to make changes and additions.

Daily planning

Each day, at the end of the day, you ask yourself:

**? What do I need to do to follow through on the commit-?
ments I've made and the lessons I've learned today?**

As you answer this question, you review your day, reflect on each sales call, and turn those reflections into action plans for the future. Then, ask yourself this question:

**? What do I need to do to be thoroughly ?
prepared for tomorrow?**

This focuses you on the sales calls you'll make tomorrow, and directs your thinking to the specific preparation you'll need for each sales call.

During the course of the day, you'll find it incredibly help-ful to ask yourself, after every sales call:

? What went well? What could I do better next time? ?

These questions prompt reflection on your performance, and continually keep you focused on improving your behavior and your competencies. And that's a course of thought that will eventually lead you to become a master of the profession.

Finally, here is another question to ask yourself during the course of the day. It is one of the most powerful self-questions I have ever discovered:

**? Am I doing, right now, the most ?
effective thing I could be doing?**

Develop the habit of asking yourself that question several times in the course of the day. Consider the answer. If the answer is no, then change what you are doing and focus on something more effective. If the answer is yes, congratulations, you are on the right track.

Here's how I happened onto this question. I had the bad habit of stopping at a coffee shop and grabbing a cup of coffee immediately after a particularly bad call. If things went badly, I had to decompress at a coffee shop, sipping coffee, reading the paper, and generally feeling sorry for myself for a while. And, although I did this routinely, I did it mindlessly, not even being aware of my habit.

Then, one day, as I was sitting in a coffee shop feeling sorry for myself after a particularly frustrating call, I asked myself that question: "Am I doing, right now, the most effective thing I could be doing?" The answer, of course, was no. "I'm sitting here feeling sorry for myself when I should be out selling something." I reflected for a moment, and discovered that I routinely did that! This wasn't an isolated event; it was a pattern of behavior. Once I discovered that about myself, I set about changing it.

That question can identify simple little things and help you stay on track in the ebb and flow of a typical day. But it can also uncover major bad habits and behavior patterns that may regularly and negatively affect your performance.

Personal Improvement Questions

The personal effectiveness questions we just reviewed are based on the premise that you can choose to do things that are more effective than others. You have a choice of how to invest your sales time, and you make those decisions about that investment by following certain thinking disciplines. The focus is on the decision you make about what to do.

The questions in this section focus on you having the ability to do what you say you want to do. In other words, before you can do something, you have to be *able* to do it. If, for example, you say, "I'm going to play in a basketball game tomorrow," that is a decision that proceeds out of the first section—

what to do. It assumes, however, that you have the ability to play the game—that you can pass, dribble, shoot, and defend. It has to do with how well you can do that which you said you were going to do. The focus is on the quality of what you do.

It is one thing to say, "I'm going to call on this huge potential account." It is quite another to say, "And I'm going to be very competent in that sales call."

In this section, we are going to examine those questions that lead to your improvement in quality—in the core sales competencies that are used throughout the sales process, and which, in conjunction with your decisions as to what to do, ultimately affect your performance as a salesperson. Superstar salespeople do the right things, and then do them with quality—in the right way.

You'll notice the questions we asked ourselves in the previous section proceeded from the top down—from the general to the specific. In other words, we determined, from an annual perspective, what we wanted to do, and then broke those down into ever more specific increments.

The questions we are going to consider in this section are best created in exactly the opposite method—from the specific to the general. Let's begin at the bottom, the most specific application we can think of, and then gradually compile our responses to move to the more general.

Daily questions

Start with a sales call. After every sales call, stop for a moment or two and ask yourself the two questions with which we ended the previous section:

? What went well? What could I do better next time? ?

Remember, good thinking is asking yourself the right questions, in the right sequence, and writing down the answers. This is a great habit to develop—taking a moment after every sales call and asking and answering those two questions. As you do so, you'll uncover trends and patterns in your behavior that need to be addressed and improved. You'll also come to a more complete understanding of your strengths and how to parley them into greater results.

The act of asking and answering those questions also helps build a basic mindset that is essential for the success of a field salesperson. Notice that the focus of the questions is on your behavior—"What could I have done...."

Sooner or later, every salesperson must take responsibility for her own results. Sales is a proactive profession—we act, and our actions get reactions. If we act well, having made good choices for the investment of our sales time, we get better results. So the ultimate determinant of our success is our actions.

It seems to be such a simple truth—that our results are determined by our actions—that it hardly bears mentioning. Unfortunately, I find expressions of the lack of this mindset everywhere. In almost every company with which I become involved, there is somewhere a belief that it is someone else's problem, someone else's decisions that affect the individual's performance. As long as we consider ourselves victims, we will never shoulder the responsibility to shape and improve our own behavior, and thus positively affect our results. These questions, asked over and over, help to instill the idea deeply within our world-views that we are responsible for our actions and our results.

Having examined our performance in each sales call, we then examine the decisions and the interactions we made every day, by asking ourselves, at the end of the day:

? What could I have done more effectively today? ?

This is a broader question, which encompasses both our specific in-call behavior, and the decisions we made throughout the day. For example, we could answer with, "I really need to become better at asking questions." Or something similar to, "That road construction on I-94 is really a problem. Next time, I'm taking the surface streets."

Regardless, the answers to the question all focus on our behavior, and ascribe a future change in action. Building the habit to continually ask these questions will lead us to decisions and actions that will eventually take us to exceptional levels of performance.

Monthly review

When we dedicate one to two hours per month to our planning session, we always begin with a reflection on the previous month. The question I prefer here is this: "Did I do what I said I was going to do?" That question should be asked in general, for your overall performance for the month, but also specifically for each category in your plan. For example, if you planned for the penetration of key accounts, your question should be:

? Did I do what I said I was going to do in this account? ?

Each account should be examined.

If your plan called for the promotion of certain products or lines, then your question should be:

? Did I do what I said I was going to do with regard to this line/product/service? ?

Having answered that question, as specifically as your plan allowed, then you need to follow up with a key question:

? Why or why not? ?

This is where you uncover those actions that either contributed to or detracted from your successes. It is just as important that you identify your strengths—the answers to the "why" question, as it is that you identify your weaknesses—the answers to the "why not" question.

As you identify your strengths, you'll naturally find ways to accentuate them and bring them into play in your sales routines. For example, as a salesperson, I discovered a real strength in working with and speaking to groups of customers and prospects. That strength later came into the fore as I moved into my practice as a trainer and speaker. However, as a salesperson, having discovered that strength, I began to seek and create opportunities to speak to groups of customers. Rather than doing three presentations to three different people within an account, for example, I'd try to bring them all together into a small group. When I was selling to surgeons, rather than trying to see each individually, I'd continually organize small-scale seminars, and try to get a half of dozen of them together.

That just happened to be my particular strength. The point is that you, like me, have strengths that can be creatively brought to bear on your task of increasing the company's revenue in your accounts. The process of asking these questions, each month, will uncover those strengths.

But it will also uncover those specific areas where you need to improve your competence. I believe in basic sales competencies. A salesperson should have a minimum competence in each of the basics, or he should not have the job. Once you have achieved a minimum degree of competence at the basics, however, you are not finished. You've only just begun. Your lifelong task is now to forever improve in those competencies.

My youngest daughter, for example, likes to play basketball. You know and I know that she needs to have a minimum skill level in each of the basic competencies of basketball, or she should not be in the game. She needs to be able to dribble, pass, shoot, and defend up to a minimum standard. If not, putting her into the game will hurt the team. However, once she has attained that minimum competency, she's not done. She's only just begun. She may be able to dribble to a minimum standard, but she can't dribble as well as Michael Jordan. If she is serious about the game, she can improve for the rest of her life.

So too is it for salespeople. There are several basic competencies that we use in each and every encounter with prospects and customers. We need to have a minimum level of competence in each of them, and then forever improve in the competencies of connecting to the customer, learning about the customer, presenting to the customer, and agreeing with the customer. These four basics provide an infrastructure for continuous and never-ending improvement.

When we ask the "why not" question, we will eventually and inevitably identify the competencies in which we are most lacking.

The final question of this series is this:

? What should I do differently next month? ?

And the objective answers to that question will lead us to a commitment to personal improvement that will, in time, eventually lead us to exceptional performance.

Annual review

? What do I want to do better next year? ?

? Specifically, how do I want to become more competent ?
and capable in the coming year?

A question such as that, asked as a culmination of the monthly questions you asked and answered along the way, focuses on your professional growth, and expresses the answer in terms of your competencies. What do you want to become better at this year? Is it asking questions, time management, getting along better with your boss? You may want to use a more specific question:

? What one specific change can I make in my routines that ?
    will have the greatest effect on my performance?

Ask yourself that question, in your annual thinking and planning retreat. Think it through in depth and detail, and write the answer down. Commit yourself to a year of focused personal improvement. That's good thinking. And good thinking precedes good results. And better results are, after all, the ultimate goal for all our efforts.

Other Applications

18   I was facilitating a CEO roundtable meeting. The host CEO, whose responsibility was to create the subject for the group discussion, announced this: "Employee participation programs don't work. That's what I'd like to discuss." The 11 other CEOs sat silently.

"Let's start with a question," I said. "What are some experiences you may have had, positive or negative, with employee participation efforts?" The group responded immediately, with several vying to be the first to speak.

It wasn't until a question was posed that the individuals within that group felt they had something to contribute to the discussion. And it wasn't just any question, it was a question that was designed to stimulate their thinking, and one to which every single group member could respond.

That's a good example of one of the myriad uses of questions. Although this book has focused on the question as a sales tool, clearly the power of a question to direct and stimulate thinking, among other things, is not limited to just the job of the salesperson.

In this chapter, we'll look at just a few of these. Let's start by expanding our application from sales to other aspects of the business realm.

A good question is a powerful management tool. Used effectively, it transfers ownership of the issue from the manager to the managed, crystallizes the issue, and suggests a positive action plan. For example, we teach sales managers to meet with their charges once a month, and conduct a "KahleWay Conference." This is a structured conference between the manager and his charges in which the manager acts as a facilitator and asks questions of the salesperson. Although the questions are more involved than these, the general flow of the conversation goes this way:

? Did you do what you said you were going to do? ?

? Why or why not? ?

? What did you learn from that? ?

? What will you do differently next month? ?

Follow the effects of this series of questions. The first, "Did you do what you said you were going to do?" is a closed-ended question that requires the salesperson to evaluate her progress, make a judgment, and take a position.

The next, "Why or why not?" forces analysis that could lead to either external factors (the competition outsold me) or internal factors (I was not well prepared).

"What did you learn from that?" asks the salesperson, to draw some conclusions. "What will you do differently?" calls for a plan of action, hopefully revised in light of the lessons learned the previous month.

In this example, the manager has led the salesperson from evaluation through analysis to planning, and finally to commitment—all by using a well-structured series of questions.

This is just one example of the use of questions as a management tool. As a person who is on 300 or so flights a year, I'm rarely at the office. When I check in I'll often ask each one of my associates this question:

? Is there anything I need to know about? ?

Notice that the language of that question implies a respect for the individual in that he is perfectly capable of handling almost everything, and then selecting only those issues that require my input or provide information that is important to me. It is a good management question.

When I run a strategic planning program, for example, one of the early steps in the process involves collecting good information upon which to make the strategic decisions that will follow. The way we do that is to look at each section of the organization's business, and then to ask questions about it. These questions are recorded, and then assigned to individuals to research and propose answers. For example, if we're thinking about the competition, we could ask:

? Who are our major competitors? ?

? Why would our customers choose to ?
    do business with each of them?

If we're considering our strengths internally, we may ask,

? How do our employees feel about us? ?

In each case, we're after the answer to the question, but the question crystallizes this issue and focuses the individual's information-collecting efforts. I cannot imagine running a strategic-planning session without being guided by a series of questions. Better questions are an integral part of every strategic-planning effort.

As a consultant, I begin our sales audits with a series of open-ended questions designed to give me a sense of the culture and focus of the operation, and follow it up with a list of about 40 specific questions that uncover the details of an organization's sales system.

Every consultant has a series of questions she uses to uncover significant issues and truths in her realm of expertise. A good question is the consultant's fundamental tool.

As a professional speaker, I'm constantly creating and refining presentations. Years ago, I learned that the first step in creating a presentation is to answer the question:

? What is the single most important thing ?
    I want the audience to learn?

Early in the stages of my preparation, I'll have a telephone conference with the meeting planners in which I ask a specific series of questions designed to give me a sense of what the audience is all about. Questions are invaluable tools for someone preparing to make a presentation.

A question, or a series of questions, is the most powerful tool a facilitator has whenever he is facilitating a group discussion. It generates thinking, creates dialogue, and moves the group to resolution. It instills in everyone the feeling that they have important contributions to make, and generates positive emotions. I've used questions to facilitate groups as varied as strategic-planning sessions, CEO roundtables, sales meetings, and home Bible studies. In a home Bible study, for example, we will often read a passage of scripture, and I'll then ask these questions:

? What does this passage say? ?

? What are the implications to us? ?

? What does that mean to you? ?

The dialogue that results from these questions moves the individuals within the group from consideration of the content of the passage to a personal reflection that may include a specific action plan. In Christian terms, we've journeyed from the head to the heart, by asking appropriate questions.

For years, I trained facilitators in our local Chamber of Commerce CEO Roundtable program. I had them begin every session with a round of open-ended, nonthreatening questions. When one of the participants digressed too far off the subject, or went on for too long, I taught them to ask a question to direct that person's thinking back to the content at hand. If the conversation stalled, they were to ask a question to generate conversation. And if they lost control of the dialogue, a well-phrased question would bring everyone back. Questions are invaluable tools for a group facilitator.

A series of good questions is the ultimate dialogue-starter. In any situation in which group discussion is encouraged, a good question is the primary tool to stimulate and focus that discussion. It doesn't have to be business. At dinner or cocktail parties, for example, I'll often ask this question of the parties involved:

> **?** What is one of the most memorable **?**
> meals you have ever had?

Notice that it is a question that everyone can answer, and that the answers often tell us about the values and experiences of the individual responding. It has never failed to generate some significant conversation that often takes the dialogue to a deeper and more intimate level.

A series of good questions is also the ultimate teaching tool. It stimulates and directs the students' thinking, and engages them in the learning process. We're all familiar with the method to which Socrates lent his name: It involves the teacher asking questions of the learner, and in so doing, guides her learning. Not only can it be used one-on-one, but also as a device to set the agenda, engage the group, and focus the learning for the group.

For years, for example, I taught a Sunday School class for adults. We would agree on a subject, say, "prayer," for example. Then we'd spend one or two sessions creating the questions that came to our mind about that subject. Equipped, then, with a list of questions, we'd jointly search the scriptures to find the answers. It could take us months. But everyone was fully engaged in seeking the answers to the questions that were most important to them. A series of good questions is the foundational tool for teachers.

My Menta-Morphosis process for continuous self-improvement is, at it's heart, a series of questions that guides the learner from a situation of discontent, through a specific commitment for changed behavior, to a newly built positive habit.

A series of good questions is also the ultimate counseling tool. My wife is a crises counselor. She has discovered that her ultimate counseling tool is a well-phrased question, designed to cause the counselees to consider their own actions and the consequences and implications of them. We all have an image of the counselor with the notepad asking questions of the counselee and writing down observations on the note pad.

A good question is a powerful tool for research, affecting research into business issues, as in the strategic planning example, to myriad applications including scientific research.

Consider this: The answers precede the questions. The answers are always there, but it takes the right question to uncover them. For example, not long ago I read a news magazine story about researchers for a pharmaceutical company studying plants and compounds from the rainforest for potential new drugs. Imagine that the cure for cancer lies in the leaves of rainforest plants. That compound has been there since the beginning of time. The solution was always there. It will be uncovered when the researcher asks the right question: Does this compound have any effect on cancer?

The answer was always there. It took the right question to discover it.

I can go on and on with these examples, but you have the idea. Whenever there is a situation in which good thinking is required, whether it is in a group or just yourself, a well-phrased question is the ultimate tool.

Appendix: Better Sales Questions

Throughout the book, we've critically examined questions that have been prepared by groups of salespeople in my seminars. In this section, I've consolidated some of the best of those, and added some we haven't discussed. Here is a group of 50 better sales questions, which I recommend to you for inclusion in your routines.

1. Why are you taking time to see me now?
2. Is there anything else I should know?
3. How much are you going to spend on [my category of product] this year?

4. In regard to the kinds of products/services I sell, what are some of your most pressing challenges?

5. What are some of the implications to the company? How important is that?

6. Which of these areas holds the most interest to you?

7. If you had some issues with your current situation, which of these would be most likely to pop up on your radar screen?

8. What are the implications of that?

9. How important would that be to your company?

10. What has to change for us to do more business here?

11. What's your current situation with regard to this issue?

12. To what degree are you having to deal with [an issue that is common for this kind of organization]?

13. What are some of the challenges high on your list today?

14. What do you think?

15. How do you feel about this?

16. Where do we go from here?

17. What's the next step?

18. Anything else?

19. How does that fit for you?

20. Is this a good time to talk?

21. What are you trying to accomplish?

22. What's your situation?

23. Why is this an issue now?

24. Why are you seeing me now?

25. What would you like to see in a [x product]?

26. What prompted you to call us?

27. We just completed a project similar to this last month. The investment was [x dollar amount]. Is that about what you were thinking?

28. What are you hoping to see from us that you may not be seeing from others?

29. Oh?

30. Can you describe what's happening?

31. What are you hoping to accomplish with this?

32. Is there anything else I should know?

33. What is the most important aspect of [this product] to you?

34. Will this need to be presented to anyone else?

35. Are there any other departments that would benefit from this?

36. To which factors are you going to give the most weight?

37. Let's talk about what is important to you.

38. Good. What exactly does that mean?

39. What have you done before when you have run into similar situations?

40. What changes would you like to see us make?

41. When would the timing be better?

42. Do I understand you correctly?

43. So, in other words, [paraphrase]. Is that right?

44. How do you think the others will react to this?

45. What two or three areas would you like to see us improve upon?

46. How are we doing up to this point?

47. Is it time to go forward with this?

48. Any reason to wait any longer?
49. What will we need to do to get started?
50. What other opportunities do you see coming up in the future?

All of these questions are generic enough to fit into almost every selling situation. Practice them and see what results you create. Then use them as the starting point for your tool chest of better sales questions you create and add to for the rest of your sales career. Because, after all, a good question is your single most powerful selling tool.

Go forth and sell well!

Index

to help you find out what customers want—in a first visit, 113-123

to help you find out what customers want—in a specific opportunity, 125-131

to help you follow up, 133-139

questions,
a better sales, 31-42
all-purpose, 69-70
daily, 192-194
edit your, 51-55
personal effectiveness, 185-191
personal improvement, 191-197
rapport and perceptive, 167
the importance of asking better, 15

R

rapport
and appearance, 164-165
and disarming honesty,166
and humor, 166
and perceptive questions, 167
and personal connection, 168
and personal story, 168
and reflective behavior, 167
and sincere compliments, 166-167

rapport, creating, 163-168

reading nonverbal communication, 176-177

reciprocity, law of, 169-170

relationship, the depth of customer, 35-36

relationships, series of questions to enhance, 25

respond positively, 178

retreat, annual thinking and planning, 186-187

review,
annual, 196-197
monthly, 194-196

S

sales questions and self questions, 17-19

satisfaction, questions to help you ensure, 151-160

self questions and sales questions, 17-19

session, monthly planning, 187-189

situation, describing the, 44-45

solutions, offering, 138

story, rapport and personal, 168

superficial leading to personal, 60-61

About the Author

Dave Kahle is a high-energy, high-content sales educator, with a special gift for engaging his audiences and stimulating people to think. A world-class speaker, he has presented in 46 states and seven countries.

Dave has honed his message through real-life experience. The number-one salesperson nationwide for two different companies in two distinct industries, he took a new territory to number one in the nation in five short years. As the general manager of a start-up company, he directed its growth from $10,000 in monthly sales to more than $200,000 in just 38 months.

His programs are powerful and career-changing because he combines his unique understanding of proven educational principles with 30 years of exceptionally successful sales experience.

Since 1988, he has served as president of The DaCo Corporation, a sales consulting and sales training firm. Dave has trained thousands of salespeople, and has authored seven books. *Ten Secrets of Time Management for Salespeople* (Career Press) has been translated into seven languages. He writes a weekly Ezine for salespeople called "Thinking About Sales."

He holds a bachelor of arts degree from the University of Toledo, and a master's degree from Bowling Green State University. He and his wife split their time between Grand Rapids, Michigan, and Sarasota, Florida.

Business Reference Essentials
From
Career Press

Business Letters for Busy People
4th Edition
John Carey
EAN 978-1-56414-612-0

Financial Statements
Thomas Ittleson
EAN 978-1-56414-341-9

The New Rules of International Negotiation
Catherine Lee
EAN 978-1-56414-973-2

Quick & Painless Business Writing
Susan F. Benjamin
EAN 978-1-56414-900-8

Winning Government Contracts
Malcolm Parvey
EAN 978-1-56414-975-6

The Small Business Owner's Manual
Joe Kennedy
EAN 978-1-56414-813-1

Sales Essentials From Career Press

10 Secrets of Time Management for Salespeople
Gain the Competitive Edge and
Make Every Second Count
Dave Kahle
EAN 978-1-56414-630-4

Barry Farber's Guide to Handling Sales Objections
Barry J. Farber
EAN 978-1-56414-773-8

6 Habits of Highly Effective Teams
Stephen Kohn & Vincent O'Connell
EAN 978-1-56414-927-5

Ask the Right Questions, Hire the Best People
Ron Fry
EAN 978-1-56414-892-6

Bridging the Generation Gap
How to Get Radio Babies, Boomers, Gen Xers,
and Gen Yers to Work Together And Achieve More
Linda Gravett & Robin Throckmorton
EAN 978-1-56414-898-8

All-Star Sales Teams
8 Steps to Spectacular Success Using Goals, Values, Vision,
and Rewards
Dan Kleinman
EAN 978-1-56414-991-6